IMPROVING ORGANIZATIONAL EFFECTIVENESS

MICHAEL ARMSTRONG

KOGAN
PAGE

First published in 1994

Kogan Page Limited
120 Pentonville Road
London N1 9JN

British Library Cataloguing in Publication Data

A CIP record for this book is available from the British Library.

ISBN 0 7494 1232 1

Typeset by Saxon Graphics Ltd, Derby
Printed in England by Clays Ltd, St Ives plc

Contents

Other books by Michael Armstrong

In his best-selling books, Michael Armstrong shows how to translate theory into effective action. Easily accessible and jargon-free, his highly-acclaimed books have become essential reading for students and all levels of management. They include:

A Handbook of Management Techniques (Second Edition)
A description of the systematic and analytical methods used by managers to assist in decision making and improve efficiency: the ideal reference work.
624pp Paperback ISBN 0 7494 1205 4; Hardback ISBN 0 7494 0702 6

A Handbook of Personnel Management Practice (Fourth Edition)
Every aspect of the personnel management function is covered in this detailed handbook which closely follows the syllabus of the Institute of Personnel Management Diploma.
976pp Paperback ISBN 0 7494 0226 1

How To Be an Even Better Manager (Fourth Edition)
A practical guide for managers and supervisors, as well as recommended reading on many business courses.
352pp Paperback ISBN 0 7494 0293 8
Also available on cassette: ISBN 0 7494 1087 6

Human Resource Management: Strategy and Action
(A fully revised edition of *Handbook of Human Resource Management*)
"Covers all aspects of the personnel function and is written in a clear and informed style." (*Management Review*)
232pp Paperback ISBN 0 7494 0714 X

Performance Management
The issues and practicalities surrounding the basis, design, development, introduction, counselling and monitoring of a successful performance management system are covered in this detailed guide.
256pp Paperback ISBN 0 7494 1242 3

Readymade Business Forms
Specimens of more than 180 of the most commonly-used forms which are easily photocopiable, and can be adapted for a company's particular needs.
272pp Paperback ISBN 0 7494 0466 3

A Handbook of Remuneration Strategy & Practice (with Helen Murlis)
"Both topical and professional . . . this is a first class reference book." (*Personnel Management*)
592pp Paperback ISBN 0 7494 1009 4

Strategies for Human Resource Management
A Total Business Approach — Edited by Michael Armstrong
Writing with human resource specialists from Coopers & Lybrand, Armstrong assesses the problems and issues in developing an integrated and effective HR strategy.
272pp Hardback ISBN 0 7494 0537 6

Preface

This book is about improving organizational effectiveness through people, recognizing that, as Peter Drucker[1] has put it: 'People determine the performance capacity of an organization.' It examines initially the concept of organizational effectiveness and the factors contributing to its achievement. Reference is made to the prescriptions of some of the more significant 'gurus' who have contributed to the generation of new concepts of management over the last decade or so.

The major areas involving people in which organizations can take steps to improve their performance, obtain added value from their human resources and achieve sustainable competitive advantage are then examined.

The book has been written within the context of the major changes that have been taking place in the environments in which organizations operate. Externally they include global competition on price, quality, innovation and service delivery. Internally they are concerned with major changes in the ways in which organizations are structured, the impact of new technology (which is at last really making its presence felt), changes in the way in which people are employed (the human resource management movement is no more than a symptom of a number of interrelated causes) and new paradigms or mindsets on how organizations and their members should be managed.

The debate on how these changes should be dealt with have produced many prescriptions and panaceas from academics, writers, consultants and managers. Some of this has been based on the thorough research and analysis of good practice. Much of it, however, has too easily degenerated into slick pontifications. Quick fixes for use in a complex world proliferate.

Clearly, in examining the factors contributing to organizational effectiveness, this book will be providing guidelines on the approaches which can be used. But these will not be prescriptions in the sense of infallible recipes for success. Organizational effectiveness is a function of a mix of factors, and the right mix will depend on the particular needs and circumstances of the organization, including its purpose, its competitive position, its technology, the management style, the sort of people employed and its culture. In one sense a menu will be provided, but the choice of items on that menu will be determined by a wide range of considerations which will be particular to individual organizations and managers.

New prescriptions for effective management such as business process re-engineering and benchmarking appear to offer solutions in organisational effectiveness, but they can only operate well within the context of an overall approach, as described in this book.

Reference

1. Drucker, P (1990) *Managing the Non-profit Organization*, Butterworth-Heinemann, Oxford.

1

What is an effective organization?

An effective organization can broadly be defined as one that makes the best use of its resources to attain high levels of performance, thus successfully achieving its purpose and objectives while also meeting its responsibilities to its stakeholders. These stakeholders consist of:

- the owners, shareholders, public authorities or trustees who direct or fund the organization;
- the employees who run the organization and carry out the activities required to achieve targets and standards of performance and delivery;
- the customers, clients or members of the public for whom the organization provides goods or services;
- the third parties such as suppliers or providers through or with whom the organization does business;
- the community in which the organization operates.

FACTORS CONTRIBUTING TO ORGANIZATIONAL EFFECTIVENESS

There is no single factor or mix of factors which will guarantee organizational effectiveness, but the following is a selection of factors which, in one way or other, will contribute to success:

- clearly defined goals and strategies to accomplish them;
- a value system which emphasizes performance, productivity, quality, customer service, teamwork and flexibility;
- strong visionary leadership from the top;
- a powerful management team;
- a well-motivated, committed, skilled and flexible workforce;

- effective teamwork throughout the organization, with win/lose conflict well under control;
- continuous pressure to innovate and grow;
- the ability to respond fast to opportunities and threats;
- the capacity to manage, indeed thrive, on change;
- a sound financial base and good systems for management accounting and cost control.

PRESCRIPTIONS FROM THE GURUS

Richard Beckhard

Richard Beckhard[1] defined a healthy organization, from a behavioural scientist's point of view, as having the following characteristics:

- the total organization, the significant subparts, and individual employees manage their work against goals and plans for the achievement of goals;
- form follows function – the problem, task or project determines how human resources are organized;
- decisions are made by or near the sources of information;
- managers and supervisors are rewarded not only in relation to short-term profit or production performance but also for developing their subordinates and creating an effective working group;
- communication laterally and vertically is relatively undistorted;
- people are open and confronting;
- there is a minimum amount of win/lose activity between individuals and groups;
- conflict (clash of ideas) may exist about tasks and projects but relatively little energy is wasted on interpersonal difficulties.

Peter Drucker

Management by objectives

Peter Drucker[2] achieved fame many years ago by inventing the concept of management by objectives. He emphasized that objectives in a business enterprise enable management to explain, predict and control activities in a way which single ideas like profit maximization do not. He identifies five key characteristics of objectives.

1. They enable the organization to explain the whole range of business phenomena in a small number of general statements.

2. They allow the testing of these statements in actual experience.
3. They enable behaviour to be predicted.
4. They facilitate the examination of the soundness of decisions while they are still being made rather than after they fail.
5. They provide for performance in the future to be improved as a result of the analysis of past experience.

Efficiency and effectiveness

In a later book Drucker[3] pointed out that to concentrate on efficiency rather than effectiveness could be limiting and therefore dangerous. It can result in:

- doing things right rather than doing right things;
- solving problems rather than producing creative alternatives;
- safeguarding resources rather than optimizing resource utilization;
- lowering costs rather than increasing profit;
- minimizing risk rather than maximizing opportunities.

Organization

On the coming of the new organization, Peter Drucker[4] has suggested that the typical organization of the future will be knowledge-based, composed largely of specialists who direct and discipline their own performance through organized feedback from colleagues, customers and headquarters.

The information-based organization of 20 years hence will have fewer than half the levels of management of its counterpart today, and no more than a third of the managers. He noted that in many organizations 'whole layers of management neither make decisions nor lead. Instead, their main, if not their only function is to serve as "relays" – human boosters for the faint, unfocused signals that pass for communication in the traditional pre-information organization.'

This creates a number of critical problems, namely:

- developing rewards, recognition and career opportunities for specialists;
- creating unified vision in an organization of specialists;
- devising the management structure for an organization of task forces;
- ensuring the supply, preparation and testing of top management people.

Charles Handy

Charles Handy[5] has suggested that an effective organization is a learning organization, which has a formal way of asking questions, seeking out theories, testing them and reflecting upon them. The questions include the following.

■ What are its strengths, talents and weaknesses?
■ What sort of organization does it want to be?
■ What does it want to be known for?
■ How does it plan to achieve it?

On organization structure, Charles Handy believes the trend is for there to be not one workforce but three: the core, the contractual fringe and the flexible labour force. Businesses, he says, are trying to get the best of both worlds: size, to give them clout in the market place and economies of scale, and small units to give them the flexibility they need as well as the 'sense of community for which individuals increasingly hanker'.

He has also forecast the growth of the federal organization. This takes the process of decentralization one stage further by establishing each key operational, manufacturing or service provision activity as a distinct, federated unit. Each federal entity runs its own affairs, although they are linked together by the overall strategy of the organization and, if it is a public company, are expected to make an appropriate contribution to corporate profitability in order to provide the required return on their shareholders' investments and to keep external predators at bay.

The centre in a federal organization maintains a low profile. The federated activities are expected to provide the required initiative, drive and energy. The centre is at the middle of things, not at the top. It is not just a banker but it does provide resources. Its main role is to coordinate, advise, influence, suggest and help to develop integrated corporate strategies.

Sir John Harvey-Jones

Sir John Harvey-Jones[6] has made the following suggestions – among many others – on the approaches adopted by successful businesses:

■ nothing will happen unless everyone down the line knows what they are trying to achieve and gives of their best to achieve it;
■ the whole of business is about taking an acceptable risk;

■ the process of deciding where you are taking the business is the opportunity to get the involvement of others, which actually forms the motive power that at the end of the day will make it happen.

Rosabeth Moss Kanter

Rosabeth Moss Kanter[7] has emphasized the importance of managing change. She believes that managers must become 'change masters, helping and guiding the organization, its management and all who work in it to manage and, indeed, to exploit and triumph over change'. Kanter has also recorded how Apple Computer devised a three-pronged approach to improving organizational effectiveness as follows.

1. Develop an organizational structure that produces synergies, not conflict.
2. Create more cooperative alliances with suppliers and customers.
3. Find ways to maintain a flow of new ideas towards new products and new ventures.

She notes[8] that American corporations are being pushed in ever less bureaucratic and ever more entrepreneurial directions, cutting out unnecessary layers of the hierarchy and forging closer ties with employees. She emphasizes, however, that the pursuit of excellence has multiplied the number of demands on executives and managers.

Rosabeth Moss Kanter has described this as the 'post-entrepreneurial corporation'. This represents a triumph of process over structure. She suggests that relationships and communication, and the flexibility temporarily to combine resources, are more important than the formal channels and reporting relationships represented in an organization chart: 'What is important is not how responsibilities are divided but how people can pull together to pursue new opportunities.'

J Katzenbach and D Smith

In *The Wisdom of Teams*, Katzenbach and Smith[9] suggested that high performing organizations have the following characteristics:

■ the primary purpose of top management is that of focusing on performance and the teams that will deliver it;
■ there is a strong and balanced performance ethic which creates and pursues the performance challenges that create effective teams;
■ to sustain a balanced performance ethic they deliver superior value to their customers, which in turn generates both attractive returns for the company's owners and personal growth opportuni-

ties and attractive earnings for employees, who, of course, are responsible for delivering superior value to customers.

Richard Pascale and Anthony Athos

The analysis of the art of Japanese management conducted by Richard Pascale and Anthony Athos[10] suggested that there are seven Ss for success, which are:

- **strategy** – the plan to reach identified goals;
- **structure** – the characteristics of the organization's structure – functional, decentralized etc;
- **systems** – the routines for processing and communicating information;
- **staff** – the categories of people employed;
- **style** - how managers behave in achieving the organization's goals;
- **skills** – the capabilities of key people;
- **superordinate goals** – the significant meanings of guiding concepts with which an organization imbues its members (ie its values).

They also made the following perceptive comment on the clash between idealism and reality in organizations:

> The inherent preferences of organizations are clarity, certainty and perfection. The inherent nature of human relationships involves ambiguity, uncertainty and imperfection.

Richard Pascale

In *Managing on the Edge*, Richard Pascale[11] suggested a new 'paradigm' for organizations in which they are:

- placing increased emphasis on the 'soft' dimensions of style and shared values;
- operating as networks rather than hierarchies;
- moving from the status-driven view that managers think and workers do as they are told, to a belief in managers as 'facilitators' with workers empowered to initiate improvements and change;
- placing less emphasis on vertical tasks within functional units, and more on horizontal tasks and collaboration across units;
- focusing less on content and the prescribed use of specific tools and techniques, and more on 'process' and a holistic synthesis of techniques;

■ changing the military model to a commitment model.

Tom Peters and Robert Waterman

From their research into 75 highly regarded enterprises, Tom Peters and Robert Waterman[12] identified the following eight attributes which characterize the excellent companies.

1. **A bias for action** The excellent companies get on with it. They are analytical in their decision making but this does not paralyse them, as it does some companies.

2. **Close to the customer** They get to know their customers, and provide them with quality, reliability and service.

3. **Autonomy and entrepreneurship** Leaders and innovators are fostered and given scope.

4. **Productivity through people** They really believe that the basis for quality and productivity gain is in the rank and file. They do not just pay lip-service to the slogan 'People are our most important asset'. They do something about it by encouraging commitment and getting everyone involved.

5. **Hands-on, value-driven** The people who run the organization get close to those who work for them, and ensure that the organization's values are understood and acted upon.

6. **Stick to the knitting** The successful organizations stay reasonably close to the businesses they know.

7. **Simple form, lean staff** The organization structure is simple and corporate staff are kept to a minimum.

8. **Simultaneous loose–tight properties** They are both decentralized and centralized. They push decisions and autonomy as far down the organization as they can get into individual units and profit centres. But, as Peters and Waterman say, 'they are fanatic centralists around the few core values they hold dear'.

However, some of the 'excellent' companies included in this study have not done so well subsequently.

Tom Peters

In *Thriving on Chaos* Tom Peters[13] commented that although many organizations have nominally decentralized (on paper) they have become re-centralized because of such factors as the dominance of finance staff with their complex centralized control systems and the demand for the central coordination of advertising budgets. More layers of management were added and expert central staffs made '(1) more requests to the line for reports, and (2) more requests that this or that report be coordinated with numerous others'. At the same time, Peters comments, the 'matrix' organization on the US National Aeronautics and Space Administration (NASA) lines became popular: 'yet another form of *de facto* centralization which attempted to gain synergies that would come from coordinating everything and everyone with everything else and anyone else'.

Against this background, he proposes the following approaches:

- break organizations into the smallest possible independent units;
- give every employee a business person's strong sense of revenue, cost and profit;
- ever-closer involvement with the customer;
- minimize management layers – no more than five in very complex organizations, three in smaller, less complex organizations with, at supervisor level, spans of control of from 25 to 75 people;
- achieve flexibility by empowering people;
- learn to love change by a new view of leadership at all levels;
- pursue fast-paced innovation.

The visible presence of 'new, flexible competitors', the need to respond to change, challenge and uncertainty, and the impact of new technology, have all combined to emphasize the need for flexibility and teamwork. The processes of federalizing and flattening organizations (stripping out layers of middle management) have added to this emphasis.

Peters also suggests that new flexible manufacturing systems and the decentralized availability of the information needed for fast product changeover are leading to the wholesale adoption of cellular manufacturing, 'which eventually concentrates all the physical assets needed for making a product in a self-contained configuration which is tailor-made for team organization'. His prescription for the new model organization is:

- the creation of self-managing teams, responsible for their own support activities such as budgeting and planning;
- managers who act as 'on call' experts, spending most of their time helping teams;

- managers who encourage constant front-line contact among functions;
- the use of small units – 'small within big' – configurations everywhere.

Peter Wickens

Peter Wickens[14] describes the three components of the Nissan 'tripod' for success as being:

- flexibility;
- quality consciousness;
- teamwork.

PURSUING ORGANIZATIONAL EFFECTIVENESS

There seems to be a bewildering number of prescriptions for organizational success. There are, however, a number of common threads running through them, including the emphasis on flatter, leaner, simpler and more decentralized or federalized organizations with smaller units which operate more flexibly.

The rest of this book explores these and other approaches to organizational effectiveness.

References

1. Beckhard, R (1969) *Organization Development: Strategy and Models*, Addison-Wesley, Reading, Mass.
2. Drucker, P (1955) *The Practice of Management*, Heinemann, London.
3. Drucker, P (1967) *The Effective Executive*, Heinemann, London.
4. Drucker, P (1988) 'The coming of the new organization', *Harvard Business Review*, January–February.
5. Handy, C (1989) *The Age of Unreason*, Business Books, London.
6. Harvey-Jones, J (1988) *Making it Happen*, Collins, Glasgow.
7. Kanter, R M (1984) *The Change Masters*, Allen & Unwin, London.
8. Kanter, R M (1989) *When Giants Learn to Dance*, Simon & Schuster, London.
9. Katzenbach, J and Smith, D (1993) *The Magic of Teams*, Harvard Business School Press, Boston, Mass.
10. Pascale, R and Athos, A (1981) *The Art of Japanese Management*, Simon & Schuster, New York.

11. Pascale, R (1990) *Managing on the Edge*, Viking, London.
12. Peters, T and Waterman, R (1982) *In Search of Excellence*, Harper & Row, New York.
13. Peters, T (1988) *Thriving on Chaos*, Macmillan, London.
14. Wickens, P (1987) *The Road to Nissan*, Macmillan, London.

ORGANIZATIONAL EFFECTIVENESS CHECKLIST

Performance indicators

1. What are the current figures and trends in the key performance areas:

   — return on capital employed;
   — earnings per share;
   — price earnings (P/E) ratio;
   — return (profit) on sales;
   — asset turnover (ratio of sales to fixed and current assets);
   — overhead ratio (ratio of overheads or expenses to sales or income);
   — cost per unit of output;
   — liquidity (ratio of current assets to current liabilities);
   — gearing (ratio of long-term loans to shareholders' funds);
   — debtors (ratio of sales to debtors);
   — inventory (stockturn – the ratio of sales to stock);
   — productivity (ratio of sales, units produced of added value to number of employees);
   — market share;
   — quality (eg percentage defects);
   — customer service (eg speed of response, delivery on time, number of justifiable complaints);
   — external opinion and reputation (the City, media etc);
   — internal opinion (how employees feel about the organization)?

Overall analysis (SWOT (strengths, weaknesses, opportunities and threats) analysis)

2. What are the internal strengths and weaknesses of the organization? Consider under the headings of:

   — product quality;
   — product maturity;
   — product availability;
   — human resources – quality, skill base, motivation, commitment, availability, retention rate, employee relations climate;
   — financial resources – capital, reserves, cash flow;
   — cost structure;
   — market share;
   — brand strength;
   — customer loyalty;
   — customer service;
   — innovative ability;
   — entrepreneurial ability;
   — flexibility;
   — responsiveness.

3. What are the external opportunities and threats facing the organization? Consider under the headings of:

   — economic factors – exchange and interest rates, inflation, growth rates, fiscal changes;
   — government influences – regulation, deregulation, availability of funds;
   — market trends – consumers' behaviour;
   — scope for new products or services (diversification);
   — scope for new or extended markets;
   — competitors' behaviour (nationally and internationally) – expansion, aggressive marketing, new products, cost cutting, service improvements, new processes, mergers, purchasing power;
   — supply factors – cost of materials and services, availability of skills, availability of energy and materials;

— social factors – environmental concerns, health and safety, equal opportunity;
— Europe – European Community (EC) regulations and initiatives.

Strategic management

4. Does the organization have a well-defined and properly communicated mission statement?
5. Does the organization understand the critical issues it faces (as identified by a SWOT analysis) and have they been articulated?
6. Has top management a clear vision of the future of the organization and the directions they want it to go?
7. Is this sense of direction translated into positive declarations of intent, and statements of the organization's goals and the plans necessary to accomplish them?
8. Are steps taken to ensure that top management's vision is shared with members of the organization?
9. Are employees encouraged to contribute to the formulation of strategies?

Organization

10. To what extent does the organization's structure help or hinder the achievement of corporate goals?
11. Is the structure appropriate to the needs of the organization, for example, to be close to the customer?
12. Are there any weaknesses in the structure such as:

— over-centralization or decentralization;
— too many layers;
— inflexibility;
— illogical grouping of activities;
— duplication of responsibility;
— lack of clarity in roles, accountabilities or reporting relationships?

Culture

13. What are the values of the organization in such fields as performance, quality, customer service, team-work, providing scope for individual responsibility and development?
14. Have these values been articulated?
15. What steps are being taken to ensure that values are upheld?
16. What are the norms (accepted ways of behaviour) in the organization in such areas as how people are treated, the work ethic, the importance attached to status, formality, the exercise of power or the accept-ability of internal politics as a way of life?
17. Should any of these norms be changed and, if so, how?
18. What is the organization climate – the working atmosphere – as expressed by the views of the employees about the organization?
19. Is the prevailing management style autocratic (management by command), democratic (manage-ment by consent) or permissive (letting things slide)?
20. What steps are necessary, if any, to improve the orga-nization's climate or its management style?

Managing change

21. What are the most important changes likely to take place in the organization's strategies, structure, activ-ities and processes, systems, and employment poli-cies and practices?
22. What is the likely impact of any changes?
23. How can any detrimental effects of change be mini-mized?

Empowerment

24. To what extent have employees been empowered in the sense that a reasonable degree of scope and free-dom has been devolved to them to exercise responsi-bility and use their abilities to the full?

25. What steps, if any, need to be taken to increase empowerment?

Leadership

26. What is the quality of leadership at the top and at other levels in the organization?

Motivation

27. How well are employees motivated to achieve higher levels of performance?
28. Is proper use being made of reward processes, both financial and non-financial, to enhance motivation?

Commitment

29. How well committed are employees to the organization and its goals?
30. What steps, if any, are required to increase commitment?

Teamwork

31. How well do individuals and teams work together in the organization?
32. How well do teams within the organization function?
33. What steps, if any, are required to improve teamwork?

Flexibility

34. Are the organization's structures, processes and systems flexible enough to deal with changing conditions and demands?
35. Are individuals generally flexible enough in terms of attitude and skill to expand or change their roles within teams, or in response to new demands?

Conflict

36. How much win/lose activity is prevalent in the organization?
37. Is conflict between individuals or teams damaging the interests of the organization?

Resourcing

38. What is the quality of employees at the various levels in the organization?
39. Has the organization an adequate skill base to meet present and future needs?
40. Are there any categories of employees who are difficult to attract and retain? If so, why?

Continuous improvement

41. What steps, if any, are being taken to ensure that the organization is functioning as a 'learning organization', ie one which facilitates the learning of all its members and continually transforms itself?
42. To what extent is a policy of continuous development applied in the organization, ie training and development regarded as a continuous process which integrates learning and work, and increases the requirement for employees to be responsible for their own learning, albeit with guidance and encouragement from the organization?

Performance management

43. Are there performance management processes within the organization which use performance goals, measurement, feedback and recognition as means of motivating employees?
44. Are performance management processes reinforced by pay-for-performance systems which clearly relate reward to contribution?

Productivity

45. Are steps being taken to improve productivity, where necessary?

Quality management

46. Is there full awareness of the need to adopt a total quality management approach, and is the thrust for improved quality driven by processes, systems and organization which make required improvements possible?

Customer care

47. Are customer care programmes in place which concentrate on improving the levels of service provided by the organization?

Managing new technology

48. Is the organization taking steps to deal with the human implications of developments in information technology, and computerized manufacturing and control systems?

Human resource management

49. Have coherent human resource strategies in the fields of resourcing, performance management, reward, continuous development and employee relations been developed which are mutually supportive and contribute to the attainment of corporate strategies?
50. Are there effective processes for involving employees in decision making on matters affecting them and obtaining their contributions on methods of improving performance?

2
Managing strategically

To provide for a successful long-term future organizations must have a purpose in life, a sense of direction and an idea of the resources they will need. They do this by managing strategically. This requires managers to understand the nature of strategy, to use strategic management processes and to prepare strategic plans, while recognizing that strategy is constantly evolving and adapting to changing circumstances.

STRATEGY – AIM AND PURPOSE

The overall aim of strategy at corporate level will be to match or fit the organization to its environment in the most advantageous way possible.

Strategy defines where the organization wants to go to fulfil its purpose and achieve its mission. It provides the framework for guiding choices which determine the organization's nature and direction. These choices relate to the organization's products or services, markets, key capabilities, growth, return on capital and allocation of resources. A strategy is therefore a declaration of intent; it defines what the organization wants to become in the longer term.

Strategies form the basis for strategic management and the formulation of strategic plans.

STRATEGIC MANAGEMENT

Strategic management is the process of formulating strategies and managing the organization to achieve them.

Organizations and managers who think and act strategically are looking ahead, and defining the direction in which they want to go in the middle and longer term. Although they are aware of the fact that businesses, like managers, must perform well in the present to succeed in the future, they are concerned with the broader issues which they are facing and the general direction in which they must go to deal with these issues.

Strategic management takes place within the context of the mission of the organization, and a fundamental task of strategic management will be to ensure that the mission is defined and relevant to the basic purpose of the organization within its changing environment. Strategic management is concerned with both ends and means. As an end, it describes a vision of what the organization will look like in a few years' time; as means, it shows how it is expected that the vision will be realized. Strategic management is therefore visionary management, concerned with creating and conceptualizing ideas of where the organization is going. But it must be translatable into empirical management, which decides how, in practice, it is going to get there.

Strategic management creates a perspective which people can share, and which guides their decisions and actions. The focus will be on identifying the organization's mission and goals, but attention is also concentrated on the resource base required to make it succeed. It is always necessary to remember that strategy is the means to create value. Managers who think strategically will have a broad and long-term view of where they are going. But they will also be aware that they are responsible first for planning how to allocate resources to opportunities which contribute to the implementation of strategy and, second, for managing these opportunities in ways which will significantly add value to the results achieved by the organization.

Key concepts in strategic management

The key concepts used in strategic management are as follows.

- **Distinctive competence** – working out what the organization is best at and what its special or unique capabilities are.
- **Focus** – identifying and concentrating on the key strategic issues.
- **Sustainable competitive advantage** – as formulated by Michael Porter[1], this concept states that to achieve competitive advantage, firms should create value for their customers, select markets where they can excel and present a moving target to their competitors by continually improving their position. Three of the most important factors are innovation, quality and cost reduction.

■ **Synergy** – developing a product market posture with a combined performance which is greater than the sum of its parts.
■ **Environmental scanning** – scanning the internal and external environment of the firm to ensure that its management is fully aware of its strengths and weaknesses, and the threats and opportunities it faces (SWOT analysis).
■ **Resource allocation** – understanding the human, financial and material resource requirements of the strategy, and ensuring that the resources are made available and their use is optimized.

FORMULATING STRATEGIES

As Henry Mintzberg[2] has pointed out, strategy formulation is not necessarily a rational and continuous process. He believes that while most of the time management pursues a given strategic orientation, changes in strategies, when they do occur, happen in brief quantum loops. In practice, 'a realized strategy can emerge in response to an evolving situation'.

Lester Dignam[3] also believes that strategy making is not always a rational, step-by-step process. He suggests that most strategic decisions are event-driven, not programmed. They are expressed as preferences rather than as exercises in applied logic. Strategy formulation, according to Dignam, is about correct decision making, not about the formulation of detailed plans. The most effective strategists are usually creative, intuitive people, employing an adaptive and flexible process.

There is a lot of truth in what Dignam says, but there are still strong arguments for adopting a systematic approach to the formulation of strategic plans, as described below.

STRATEGIC PLANNING

Strategic planning is a systematic, analytical approach which reviews the business as a whole in relation to its environment with the object of:

■ developing an integrated, coordinated and consistent view of the route the organization wishes to follow;
■ facilitating the adaption of the organization to environmental change.

The aim of strategic planning is to create a viable link between the organization's objectives and resources, and its environmental opportunities.

FORMULATING STRATEGIC PLANS

A systematic approach to formalizing strategic plans consists of the following steps.

1. **Define the organization's mission** – its overall purpose.
2. **Set objectives** – definitions of what the organization must achieve to fulfil its mission.
3. **Conduct environmental scans** – internal appraisals of the strengths and weaknesses of the organization, and external appraisals of the opportunities and threats which face it (a SWOT analysis).
4. **Analyse existing strategies** – determining their relevance in the light of the environmental scan. This may include gap analysis to establish the extent to which environmental factors might lead to gaps between what is being achieved and what could be achieved if changes in existing strategies were made. In a corporation with a number of distinct businesses, an analysis of the viability of each strategic business unit (portfolio analysis) can take place to establish strategies for the future of each unit.
5. **Define strategic issues** in the light of the environmental scan, the gap analysis and, where appropriate, the portfolio analysis.
6. **Develop new or revised strategies** and amend objectives in the light of the analysis of strategic issues.
7. **Decide on the critical success factors** related to the achievement of objectives and the implementation of strategy.
8. **Prepare operational, resource and project plans** designed to achieve the strategies and meet the critical success factor criteria.
9. **Implement** the plans.
10. **Monitor results** against the plans and feed back information which can be used to modify strategies and plans.

THE PLANNING PROCESS

It is important to operate a planning process which will not only produce realistic and potentially rewarding plans, but will also secure the support of all those involved in implementing them. There are three approaches that can be adopted to strategic planning.

- **A top-down process**, in which managers are given targets to achieve which they pass on down the line.
- **A bottom-up process**, in which functional and line managers, in conjunction with their staff, submit plans, targets and budgets for approval by higher authority.

■ **An iterative process**, which involves both the top-down and bottom-up setting of targets. There is a to and from movement between different levels until agreement is reached. However, this agreement will have to be consistent with the organization's overall mission, objectives and priorities, and will have to be made within the context of the financial resources available.

The iterative approach which involves the maximum number of people is the one most likely to deliver worthwhile and acceptable strategic plans.

BENEFITS OF STRATEGIC MANAGEMENT

The benefits of strategic management are that it can:

■ provide an integrated, coordinated and accepted view of the route the organization wishes to follow;
■ facilitate the adaptation of the organization to environmental change;
■ ensure that proper consideration is given to the financial, human and physical resources required in the future.

References

1. Porter, M (1985) *Competitive Advantage: Creating and Sustaining Superior Performance,* Free Press, New York.
2. Mintzberg, H (1987) 'Crafting strategy', *The Harvard Business Review*, July–August.
3. Dignam, L (1990) *Strategic Management: Concepts, Decisions, Cases,* Irwin, New York.

STRATEGIC MANAGEMENT CHECKLIST

Mission

1. What is the mission of the organization?
2. Is there a mission statement which:

    — focuses attention on purpose – what the organization is there to do;
    — conveys the vision of top management about the future of the organization;
    — provides a foundation upon which strategic plans can be made;

— leads to the development of explicit statements defining the core values of the organization.

3. Does the mission statement comply with the following requirements?

   — It should have 'personality', in other words, it should reflect the realities of the organization and should not simply consist of bland pieces of prose brought down from the shelf.
   — There should be top management consensus about the statement and commitment to its message.
   — The formulation of the mission statement should go hand-in-hand with definitions of core values, strategies and critical success factors – what the organization intends to do, the way it intends to set about doing it and the criteria for accomplishment.
   — The statement should take account of the external environment and the corporate culture.

4. Has specific action in the shape of briefings, discussions and workshops taken place to ensure that the mission statement is fully understood and acted upon throughout the organization?

Objectives

5. Has the organization clearly defined objectives under such headings as:

   — profitability, sales, overheads and other key ratios relating to liquidity, assets, gearing, debtors and inventory;
   — market share and standing;
   — innovation;
   — productivity;
   — manager performance and development;
   — employee performance and attitude;
   — public responsibility.

6. Have these objectives been defined as specific targets, wherever possible or, alternatively, as projects to be completed or standards to be obtained?

7. Do processes exist for the dissemination of these objectives to members of the organization, and for the translation of corporate objectives into departmental, functional and individual objectives?

8. Is scope provided for individuals to contribute to the formulation of their own objectives and, indeed, those of their department or function and thus, ultimately, those for the organization as a whole?

Environmental scanning

9. Have appraisals been conducted of the strengths and weaknesses of the organization, and the opportunities and threats which face it (a SWOT analysis)?

Analysis of existing strategies

10. Have existing strategies been systematically analysed in order to determine their relevance in the light of the environmental scan?

Definition of strategic issues

11. Have the strategic issues facing the organization been determined in the light of the environmental scan? This would involve asking such questions as the following.

    — How are we going to maintain growth in a declining market for our most profitable product?

    — In the face of aggressive competition, how are we going to maintain our competitive advantage and market leadership?

    — What action are we going to take as a result of the portfolio analysis of our strategic business units?

    — To what extent do we need to diversify into

new products and markets, and in which directions should we go?
— What proportion of our resources should be
allocated to research and development?
— Are we satisfied that we are making the best
use of new technology?
— What can we do about our overheads?
— How are we going to finance our projected
growth?
— How are we going to ensure that we have the
management strength and skilled workforce we
need in the future?
— How are we going to make the best use of our
distinctive competences?
— To what extent do we need to restructure the
organization?
— What steps do we need to take to improve the
commitment and motivation of our workforce?

Developing new or revised strategies

12. Have new or revised strategies and objectives been
formulated in the light of the analysis of strategic
issues?
13. Do these strategies:

— exploit opportunities and strengths revealed by
the SWOT analysis;
— deal with the threats and weaknesses revealed
by that analysis;
— take full account of projections of future trends,
and are based on reasonable assumptions;
— take into account the human and financial
resources required to take the organization
forward, and finance expansion and product or
market development;
— allow for the fact that, inevitably, changes in
the internal or external environment will mean
that the strategies and supporting plans will
have to be modified?

Critical success factors

14. Have the critical success factors relating to the achievement of objectives and the implementation of strategy been determined?
15. Do these critical success factors define clearly what needs to be done to achieve the organization's mission and cover the key performance areas such as innovation (product, market and technical development), market standing, quality, customer service, productivity and cost?

Operational, resource and project plans

16. Have realistic and potentially flexible operational, resource and project plans been designed to achieve the strategies and meet the critical success factor criteria?

Implementation

17. Have proper steps been taken to ensure that corporate plans are converted into departmental, functional and, as appropriate, individual work plans, all of which are consistent with the overall plans?
18. Have adequate steps been taken to ensure that the human, financial and physical resources required to implement the plans are available?

Monitoring results

19. Are interim and final results systematically monitored against objectives and plans, and in relation to changing circumstances?
20. Is information fed back on the basis of this internal and external monitoring process which can be used to modify strategies and plans?

3

Organization design

An effective enterprise ensures that collective effort is organized to achieve specific ends. Organization design divides the overall management task into a variety of activities and then establishes means of coordinating those activities. It is about differentiating activities in times of uncertainty and change, integrating them – grouping them together to achieve the organization's overall purpose – and ensuring that effective information flows and channels of communication are maintained.

Organization design is based on the analysis of activities, decisions, information flows and roles. It produces a structure which consists of positions and units between which there are relationships involving cooperation, the exercise of authority and the exchange of information. The structure must be appropriate to the organizational purpose and to the situation in which it exists. It must be flexible enough to adapt itself easily to new circumstances – organization design is a continuous process of modification and change, it is never a one-off event. It must also be recognized that, although the formal organization structure will define who is responsible for what and the ostensible lines of communication and control, the way in which it actually operates will depend on informal networks and other relationships which have not been defined in the design process, and arise from the day-to-day interactions of people.

THE APPROACH TO ORGANIZATION DESIGN

Organization design aims to clarify roles and relationships so far as this is possible in fluid conditions. It is also concerned with giving people the scope and opportunity to use their skills and abilities to better effect – this is the process of empowerment which is examined in Chapter 11. Jobs should be designed to satisfy the requirements of the organization for productivity, operational efficiency and quality of product or service. But they must also meet the needs of individuals for interest, challenge and accomplishment. These aims are inter-related, and an important aim of organization and job design (the latter is dealt with in Chapter 4) is to integrate the needs of the individual with those of the organization.

When it comes to designing or modifying the structure, a pragmatic approach is necessary. It is first necessary to understand the environment, the technology and the existing systems of social relationships. An organization can then be designed which is *contingent* upon the circumstances. There is always some choice, but designers should try to achieve the best fit they can. And, in making their choice, they should be aware of the structural, human and systems factors which will influence the design, and of the context within which the organization operates.

Organization design is ultimately a matter of ensuring that the structure and methods of operation fit the strategic requirements of the business and its technology within its environment. Disruption occurs if internal and external coherence and consistency is not achieved. And, as Mintzberg[1] suggests: 'Organizations, like individuals, can avoid identity crises by deciding what they wish to be and then pursuing it with a healthy obsession.'

AIM OF ORGANIZATION DESIGN

The aim of organization design is to produce a logical, coherent, cohesive, yet flexible structure which will facilitate the achievement of the organization's objectives.

A *logical* organization structure is one which:

- groups related activities appropriately together;
- is consistent with the flows of information, decision making and processing activities within the organization;
- provides a framework for operations – avoiding the duplication of activities and facilitating the allocation of accountability for results, preferably as close to the scene of action as possible;

A *coherent* structure is one in which roles and relationships are clearly defined and understood. Although there will inevitably be some need for flexibility in response to change, allowance has to be made for the fact that many people crave certainties and structure.

They are not very good at managing ambiguity.

A *cohesive* structure is one in which, although individual roles and responsibilities have been differentiated, equal attention has been given to the processes required to integrate activities.

A *flexible* structure is one which can adapt quickly to new situations, and gives teams and individuals scope to respond to new demands.

ORGANIZATIONAL DILEMMAS

In achieving these aims, however, there will always be a number of organizational dilemmas, for example:

- *both* allocating responsibilities and defining relationships clearly, *and* satisfying the need for flexibility in turbulent conditions;
- *both* instituting clear information flows, *and* allowing for the need quickly to adapt such flows in response to new demands;
- *both* building teams, *and* emphasizing individual accountability;
- *both* differentiating activities, *and* integrating them;
- *both* devolving power lower down, closer to the customer, *and* aligning activities through a central strategic thrust;
- *both* encouraging innovation and initiative, *and* achieving a reasonable degree of consistency in the implementation of policy;
- *both* grouping the responsibility for particular activities logically in individual jobs, *and* allowing for the fact that many roles will need to be shaped around the capacities of the individuals available to carry them out.

There is no easy answer to these dilemmas. It all depends on what the organization wants to achieve, the environment in which it operates, and the skills and characteristics of the people it employs.

Organization design is always an empirical and evolutionary process. It is impossible to lay down any firm principles for organization design, although there are a number of broad guidelines which should be taken into account even if they are not followed slavishly. These are listed below.

ORGANIZATION GUIDELINES

The basic organizational guidelines are as follows.

- **Allocation of work**. The work that needs to be done and accountabilities for results should be defined and allocated to the appropriate job holders or departments. Related activities should be grouped together to avoid unnecessary overlap and duplication of work. Matters requiring a decision should be dealt with as near to the point of action as possible. Managers should not try to do too much themselves. Neither should they exercise too close supervision.

■ **Levels in the structure**. Too many levels of management and supervision inhibit communication and create extra work (and unnecessary jobs). The aim should be to reduce the number of levels to a minimum. However, the elimination of middle managers and wider spans of control mean that more attention has to be paid to improving teamwork, delegation and methods of integrating activities.

■ **Span of control**. There are limits to the number of people anyone can manage or supervise well, but these vary considerably between different jobs. Most people can work with a far greater span of control than they think they can, as long as they are prepared to delegate more effectively, to avoid getting involved in too much detail and to develop good teamwork among the individuals reporting to them. In fact, wide spans of control are beneficial in that they can enforce delegation and better teamwork, and free the higher level manager to spend more time on policy making and planning. Limited spans of control encourage managers to interfere too much with the work going on beneath them and therefore constrain the scope that should be given to their subordinates to grow with their jobs.

■ **One person, one boss**. Generally speaking, individuals should be accountable only to one boss to avoid confusion on operational matters. But individuals might have to accept what can be described as 'functional authority', for example, a personnel manager will have authority to ensure that employment law requirements are met.

■ **Decentralization**. Authority to make decisions should be delegated as close to the action as possible.

■ **Optimize the structure**. Design the ideal organization by all means, but also remember that it may have to be modified to fit in the particular skills and abilities of key individuals.

■ **Relevance to organizational needs**. The organization structure has to be developed or amended to meet the needs of its situation. In today's conditions of turbulence and change this inevitably means a tendency towards more decentralized and flexible structures, with greater responsibility given to individuals and an extension of the use of task forces and project teams to deal with opportunities or threats. This implies an informal, non-bureaucratic, organic approach to organization design (ie the form of the organization will follow its function, not the other way around).

THE BASIC APPROACH TO ORGANIZATION DESIGN

The basic approach to organization design is to:

- define what the organization exists to do – its purpose and objectives;
- analyse and identify the activities or tasks required to do it and, as appropriate, the flow of decision making and work throughout the organization (this analytical process is described in detail in the next section of this chapter);
- allocate related activities to teams and individual job holders as appropriate;
- group related activities carried out by teams and individual job holders logically into organizational units;
- provide for the management and coordination of the activities at each level of responsibility;
- ensure that attention is given to developing the processes of teamwork and communication;
- establish reporting and communicating relationships;
- recognize the importance of informal networks as means of communicating information and joint decision making;
- provide, as far as possible, for organizational processes to adapt to change.

The design may be carried out within the organization or with the help of outside consultants on the grounds that the latter can bring additional objectivity to bear on the problems because they are detached from the day-to-day issues. It is most important, however, that the staff concerned should be involved in the design studies, not only because they can contribute a lot to the generation of practical solutions, but also because involvement brings about ownership and, if this is not achieved, it may be difficult to introduce changes smoothly.

ORGANIZATION ANALYSIS

Organization analysis is the process of analysing activities (the work done, and the technologies and administrative processes in use), decisions, relationships, information flows, structure and human resources in order to provide a basis for organization design or redesign.

The analysis should take place within the context of an understanding of the mission and strategies of the organization and the environment in which it operates.

Activities

Activity analysis establishes what work is carried out and what needs to be carried out if the organization is to achieve its objectives. The analysis should start with a broad look at the basic functions and technologies of the organization.

The points to be established are that everything is being done that needs to be done and nothing is being done which does not need to be done. It is also necessary to find out if the activities are being carried out in the right place and by the right people, and if there is any duplication.

Decisions

The analysis of activities and tasks leads naturally into the analysis of decisions. This aims to establish where the key decisions are made, the extent to which the authority to make decisions is shared and devolved, and the degree of centralization or decentralization of decision making.

Decision analysis is most helpful when it cuts across vertical and horizontal boundaries: vertical between levels in the hierarchy; horizontal between teams and individuals in different areas who jointly contribute to decisions affecting the whole of the organization or more than one function or department.

An important aim of decision analysis is to establish who ultimately has the authority to make policy or operating decisions. It will show who is responsible for formulating the policy guidelines which govern decision-making processes and who is contributing to the decision by providing information or advice. Some indication should be given of the division of responsibility for decisions between different levels in the hierarchy.

The decision analysis should provide a basis for questions on such matters as the extent to which decision-making authorities are clear, whether or not decisions are being made in the right place and by the right people, and the degree to which there is adequate communication and consultation during the process of making decisions.

Information flows

The analysis of information flows examines the channels of communication in the organization, and how information flows between and within departments. It identifies the key information areas, who is responsible for generating, processing and acting on the information, and how it moves through the organization or department.

Flow charts can be used to describe information routes and the actions taken at various points along the way. The analyst will establish the extent to which information flows smoothly and logically, and ensure that the organization structure reflects the flow and does not impede its progress.

Relationships

The analysis of information flows will indicate the contacts that are regularly made by individuals with colleagues, customers and outside bodies, and how networks function. The analysis should provide information on the extent to which the grouping of activities, and the relationships between departments and individuals are conducive to cooperation, the integration of activities and decision making. The relationship analysis should also establish the power structure of the organization – who exerts influence, who gets things done.

Structure

The structural analysis will be concerned with:

- how activities are grouped together;
- the extent to which functions are centralized or decentralized;
- the degree to which decision-making authority is devolved in the organization;
- the use of teams and the development of teamwork generally;
- the number of levels in the hierarchy;
- the span of control of managers;
- job structure – the range of tasks carried out in individual jobs, the grouping of tasks into jobs, the amount of responsibility and authority allocated to job holders, and the extent to which they understand what they have to do. Job design is covered in Chapter 4.

Human resources

Management and staff resources need to be analysed from two points of view: first, the extent to which the existing structure has been built round the personalities and strengths or weaknesses of the key people in the organization and, second, the availability of the quality of people required to enable any necessary changes in organization structure to take place.

ORGANIZATION PLANNING

Organization planning is the process of converting the analysis into the design. It determines structure, relationships, roles, management and staff requirements, and how changes should be implemented. The three planning steps are to:

- list and evaluate alternative approaches to the organization design and deciding what, on balance, is the best approach;
- prepare definitions of the structure and roles;
- identify problems of implementing the organization and preparing a plan for doing so.

Evaluating and deciding on the design

There is no one best design. There is always a choice between alternatives and logical analysis will help to evaluate their relative merits, but the law of the situation must prevail. The structure will be contingent on the circumstances.

It may have to be accepted that a logical regrouping of activities cannot be introduced in the short term because no one is available with the experience and ability to manage them, or because a capable individual is so firmly entrenched in a job that to uproot him or her would reduce the overall effectiveness of the revised organization structure.

One of the most difficult tasks of anyone concerned with designing or redesigning organization structures is that of reconciling ideal requirements with the practical realities of the situation. This is why, more often than not, organization structures are a compromise; but as long as they work this will not matter. And it should always be remembered that what makes organizations really effective is not so much the structure but the ability, willingness and commitment of the people in the organization to work well together to achieve a common purpose.

It is also worth bearing in mind that organizations are always in a state of evolution – environmental and technical changes and the forces of competition impose the need to alter groupings of activities and lines of communication continuously. Arrangements have to be made for introducing new activities or for removing unnecessary ones. Acquisitions and the disposal of businesses have to be catered for, and takeovers or mergers may impose an entirely new structure. The process of modifying and adjusting organization structures never stops.

The worst sins that organization designers can commit is that of imposing their own ideology on the organization, and imagining that they have the final and inevitable solution to its problems. Those concerned with the design of organizations have to be eclectic in their knowledge, sensitive in their analysis of the situation, aware of the implications of change and deliberate in their approach to the evaluation of alternatives.

Defining structures and roles

Structures can be defined by means of organization charts and roles by job descriptions. Organization charts are useful in planning and reviewing large organizations. They indicate how work is allocated and how activities are grouped together. They show who is responsible to whom and they illustrate lines of authority. Drawing up a chart can be a good way of clarifying what is currently happening: the mere process of putting the organization down on paper will highlight any problems. And when it comes to considering changes, charts are the best way of illustrating alternatives.

The danger with organization charts is that they can be mistaken for the organization itself. They are no more than a snapshot of what is supposed to be happening at a given moment. They are out of date as soon as they are drawn, and they leave out the informal organization and its networks. If you use little boxes to represent people, they may behave as if they were indeed little boxes, sticking too closely to the book of rules.

Charts can make people very conscious of their superiority or inferiority in relation to others. They can make it harder to change things, they can freeze relationships and they can show relationships as they are supposed to be, not as they are. Robert Townsend[2] said of organization charts: 'Never formalize, print and circulate them. Good organizations are living bodies that grow new muscles to meet challenges.'

Role definitions describe the part to be played by individuals in fulfilling their job requirements. Roles therefore indicate the behaviour required to carry out a particular task or the group of tasks contained in a job – they will set out the context within which individuals work as part of a team, as well as the tasks they are expected to carry out.

The traditional form of defining roles is the job description, but like organization charts, job descriptions can be too rigid and stifle initiative. It is better to use a role definition format along the following lines:

- job title;
- reporting relationships;
- main purpose of the role – a brief description of why the role exists;
- main areas of responsibility – these are defined in terms of the results expected, no attempt should be made to go into any detail of how the work is done;
- context – how the job fits in with others, flexibility requirements, decision-making authority, any particular requirements or pressures.

A role definition emphasizes the dynamic aspects of a job in terms of output, relationships and flexibility. A role description should focus on performance and delivery, not on tasks and duties.

Implementation

At the implementation stage it is necessary to ensure that everyone concerned:

- knows how they will be affected by the change;
- understands how their relationships with other people will change;
- accepts the reasons for the change and will not be reluctant to participate in its implementation.

It is easy to tell people what they are expected to do; it is much harder to get them to understand, and accept how and why they should do it. The implementation plan should therefore cover not only the information to be given but also how it should be presented. The presentation will be easier if, in the analysis and design stage, full consultation has taken place with the individuals and groups who will be affected by the change. Too many organizational changes have failed because they have been imposed from above or from outside without proper consideration for the views and feelings of those who are most intimately concerned.

Implementation is often attempted by purely formal means – issuing edicts, distributing organization manuals or handing out job descriptions. These may be useful as far as they go, but while they provide information, they do not necessarily promote understanding and ownership. This can only be achieved on an informal but direct basis. Individuals must be given the opportunity to talk about what the proposed changes in their responsibilities will involve – they should already have been given the chance to contribute to the thinking behind the change, so discussions on the implications of the proposals should follow quite naturally. There is no guarantee that individuals who feel threatened by change will accept it, however much they have been consulted. But the attempt should be made. Departmental, team and inter-functional meetings can help to increase understanding. Change management is discussed in more detail in Chapter 7.

The implementation plan may have to cater for the likelihood that all the organizational changes cannot be implemented at once. Implementation may have to be phased to allow changes to be introduced progressively, to enable people to absorb what they will be expected to do and to allow for any training required to take place. Changes may in any case be delayed until suitable people for new positions are available.

References

1. Mintzberg, H (1981) 'Organization design: fashion or fit', *Harvard Business Review*, January–February.

2. Townsend, R (1970) *Up the Organization*, Michael Joseph, London.

ORGANIZATION DESIGN CHECKLIST

Overall considerations

1. What is the mission/overall purpose of the organization?
2. Is the mission clearly defined, appropriate and well understood?

3. What is the general nature of the work carried out in the organization:

    — manufacturing – products and markets;
    — service provision – types and charts ;
    — customers or end-users;
    — sector: private, public, not-for-profit?

4. What changes are taking place in the mission and nature of the organization?

Strategies

5. What are the main business or corporate strategies?
6. How are these likely to impact on the structure of the organization?

Activities

7. What are the main activities carried out in the organization? (Quantify these activities as much as possible.)
8. Are all the activities required to meet objectives properly catered for?
9. How well are these activities coordinated and integrated?

Grouping of activities

10. On what basis are activities grouped together – by product, function, process, region, customer or client, or by a combination of any of these?
11. Is the basis for grouping logical and conducive to the coordination of activities and good communications?
12. Are there any instances of organizational units being responsible for activities which could more appropriately be carried out elsewhere?
13. Is there any scope for grouping activities more closely together to facilitate integration?
14. Is there any need for further decentralization or regionalization to bring activities into closer contact with local customers, clients, suppliers or sources of information?

15. Does the nature of the work suggest that a less formal organization making more use of networks, project teams or task forces would be appropriate?

Devolution

16. Is sufficient authority devolved close to the scenes of action?
17. Do centralized organizational functions contribute to the coordination and control of organizational policies and plans without unduly interfering with local management?
18. Is there a need for more devolution, or, conversely, more central guidance or control?

Organizational levels

19. Are there too many levels in the organization, thus inhibiting effective communications, creating unnecessary jobs, proliferating control mechanisms or hindering good teamwork?

Span of control

20. Are there any instances where managers or supervisors have more people reporting to them than they can effectively control or communicate with?
21. Are there any instances where managers or supervisors have such a small number of people reporting to them that they are interfering too much with the work of their subordinates?

Individual roles

22. Are there any cases where job holders:

   — are not clear about what they are expected to do;
   — are unsure about whom they report to for what or who reports to them;
   — are being asked to do too much in too little time;

— have insufficient time to carry out the full range of their responsibilities (eg managers who are so preoccupied with day-to-day tasks that they have no time to plan ahead or communicate with their subordinates);
— do not have the authority, resources or information which will enable them to carry out their jobs effectively;
— are carrying out a range of miscellaneous tasks which do not seem to be logically grouped together;
— are carrying out duties which are better performed elsewhere or are unnecessarily duplicated elsewhere?

23. Is there a sufficient degree of flexibility in the ways in which jobs are designed to ensure that job holders can take on new roles in response to changing demands?
24. In general, are individual job holders given sufficient scope and responsibility to use their abilities to the full?
25. To what extent and how justifiably have jobs been structured around the capacities of those holding them?

4
Job design

Job design is the process of specifying the contents and relationships of jobs in order to satisfy technological and organizational requirements, as well as the social and personal needs of the job holder.

AIMS

Job design aims to improve organizational effectiveness by both satisfying the requirements of the organization for productivity, operational efficiency and quality of product or service, and also by satisfying the needs of individuals for interest, challenge and accomplishment. These aims are interrelated, and can be achieved by the analysis and satisfaction of work requirements, structuring jobs appropriately and paying attention to the motivating characteristics of jobs.

ANALYSIS OF WORK REQUIREMENTS

The process of job design must start from an analysis of what work needs to be done – the tasks that have to be carried out if the purpose of the organization or an organizational unit is to be achieved. This is where the techniques of work study, systems and process analysis and organizational analysis are used. Inevitably, these techniques are directed to the first aim of job design: the improvement of organizational performance. They concentrate on the technical aspects of work to be done, not workers and the social system in which they carry out their roles. The task analysis techniques may lead to a high degree of task specialization and assembly line processing – of paperwork as well as physical products. This in turn can lead to the maximization of individual responsibility and the opportunity to use personal skills.

It is necessary, however, to follow Drucker and distinguish between efficiency and effectiveness. The most efficient method may maximize outputs in relation to inputs in the short run, but it may not be effective in the longer term in that it fails to achieve the overall objectives of the activity. The pursuit of short-term efficiency by imposing the maximum degree of task specialization may reduce longer term effectiveness by demotivating job holders, and increasing labour turnover and absenteeism.

Job design has therefore to start from work requirements because that is why the job exists. When the tasks to be done have been determined it should then be the function of the job designer to consider how the jobs can be set up to provide the maximum degree of motivation for those who have to carry them out. (Motivating factors in jobs are considered later in this chapter.)

STRUCTURING JOBS

Job design requires the assembly of a number of tasks into a job or a group of jobs. An individual may carry out one main task, which consists of a number of interrelated elements or functions, or task functions may be split between a team working closely together or strung along an assembly line. In more complex jobs, individuals may carry out a variety of connected tasks, each with a number of functions, or these tasks may be allocated to a group of workers or divided between them. Complexity in a job may be a reflection of the number and variety of tasks to be carried out, or the range and scope of the decisions that have to be made, or the difficulty of predicting the outcome of decisions.

The internal structure of each task consists of three elements: planning (deciding on the course of action, its timing and the resources required); executing (carrying out the plan), and controlling (monitoring performance and progress and taking corrective action when required). A completely integrated job includes all these elements for each of the tasks involved. The worker, having been given objectives in terms of output, quality and cost targets, decides on how the work is to be done, assembles the resources, performs the work, and monitors output, quality and cost standards. Responsibility in a job is measured by the amount of authority someone has to do all these things. The ideal arrangement from the point of view of motivation is to provide for fully integrated jobs containing all three task elements.

MOTIVATING FACTORS

The way in which jobs are designed will influence the degree to which they provide 'intrinsic' motivation, ie motivation from the work itself. This is related to the fundamental concept that people are motivated when they are provided with the opportunity to achieve their goals. Work provides the means to earn money, which as an extrinsic reward satisfies basic needs and is instrumental in providing ways of satisfying higher level needs. But work also provides intrinsic rewards which are under the direct control of the workers themselves.

Four characteristics are required if jobs are to provide intrinsic motivation.

1. **Feedback** Individuals must receive meaningful feedback about their performance, preferably by measuring and evaluating it themselves. This implies that they should ideally work on a complete product or a significant part of it which can be seen as a whole.
2. **Use of abilities** The job must be perceived by individuals as requiring them to use abilities they value in order to perform the job effectively.
3. **Responsibility** The job must maximize the job holder's responsibility for performance and quality.
4. **Self-control** Individuals must feel that they have a high degree of self-control over setting their own goals and over defining the paths to these goals.

These characteristics can be provided for individuals by the process of job enrichment and for teams by creating autonomous working groups and high performance work teams.

JOB ENRICHMENT

Job enrichment aims to maximize the interest and challenge of work by providing the employee with a job that has these characteristics:

- it is a complete piece of work in the sense that the worker can identify a series of tasks or activities that end in a recognizable and definable product;
- it affords the employee as much variety, decision-making responsibility and control as possible in carrying out the work;
- it provides direct feedback through the work itself on how well the employee is doing the job.

Job enrichment is not just increasing the number or variety of tasks; nor is it the provision of opportunities for job rotation. These approaches may relieve boredom, but they do not result in positive increases in motivation.

There is no one way of enriching a job. The technology and the circumstances will dictate which of the following techniques or combination of techniques is appropriate:

- increasing the responsibility of individuals for their own work;
- giving employees more scope to vary the methods, sequence and pace of their work;
- giving a person or a work group a complete natural unit of work, ie reducing task specialization;
- removing some controls from above while ensuring that individuals or groups are clearly accountable for achieving defined targets or standards;
- allowing employees more influence in setting targets and standards of performance;
- giving employees the control information they need to monitor their own performance;
- encouraging the participation of employees in planning work, introducing new techniques and reviewing results;
- introducing new and more difficult tasks not previously handled;
- assigning individuals or groups specific projects which give them more responsibility and help them to increase their expertise.

These approaches are associated with the concept of empowerment as described in Chapter 11.

AUTONOMOUS WORK GROUPS

An autonomous work group is allocated an overall task and given the maximum amount of discretion over how the work is done. This provides for intrinsic motivation by giving members of the group autonomy and the means to control their work, which will include feedback information.

An autonomous work group:

- enlarges individual jobs to include a wider range of operative skills;
- decides on methods of work, and the planning, scheduling and control of work;

■ distributes tasks itself among its members;
■ decides on work pace and when to work.

HIGH PERFORMANCE WORK GROUPS

A high performance work group takes the principles behind the autonomous work group one step further by placing greater emphasis on higher levels of performance in new technology environments. High performance work design requires the following steps.

1. Management defines what it needs in the form of new technology or methods of production and the results expected from its introduction.
2. Multiskilling is encouraged – that is, job demarcation lines are eliminated as far as possible, and encouragement and training are provided for employees to acquire new skills.
3. Equipment is selected which can be used flexibly, and is laid out to allow freedom of movement and vision.
4. Autonomous working groups are established, each with around a dozen members, and with full 'back-to-back' responsibility for product assembly and testing, fault-finding and some maintenance.
5. Managers adopt a supportive rather than an autocratic style with groups and group leaders (this is the most difficult part of the system to introduce).
6. Support systems are provided, for example, kit-marshalling and material supply in manufacturing, which help the groups to function effectively as productive units.
7. Management sets goals and standards for success.
8. The new system is introduced with great care by means of involvement and communication programmes.
9. Thorough training is carried out on the basis of an assessment of training needs.
10. The payment system is specially designed with staff participation to fit their needs as well as those of management.

JOB DESIGN CHECKLIST

1. Is adequate attention paid to designing jobs from the point of view of maximizing performance and motivation?

2. Are jobs structured on the basis of a proper analysis of task requirements?
3. Is attention paid to the need to structure jobs to incorporate the following key elements: planning, executing and control?
4. Is sufficient attention given to providing intrinsic motivation by designing jobs in a way which maximizes feedback, makes the best use of the job holder's abilities, provides the maximum degree of responsibility for performance and quality, and gives individuals a high degree of control over setting goals and planning to achieve them?
5. Have any deliberate steps been taken to use job enrichment techniques in designing jobs?
6. Is there scope for developing autonomous work groups or high performance work teams?

5

Organization development

WHAT IS ORGANIZATION DEVELOPMENT?

Organization development (OD) is concerned with the planning and implementation of programmes designed to improve the effectiveness with which an organization functions and responds to change.

The concept of organization development originated in the 1960s when the behavioural science movement came to the fore. It achieved its greatest prominence in the 1970s when 'OD' consultancies and practitioners multiplied with their prescriptions for what they often called 'organizational health'.

BASIS OF ORGANIZATION DEVELOPMENT

The basis of the original organization development programmes was provided by the behavioural science theories developed by writers such as the following.

- **Douglas McGregor**[1] who originated what he called the central principle of integration – the process of recognizing the needs of both the organization and the individual, and creating conditions which can reconcile their needs so that members of the organization work together for its success and share in its rewards: 'Man will exercise self-direction and self-control in the service of objectives to which he is committed.'
- **Rennis Likert**[2] who developed his integrating principle of supportive relationships which states that:

  The leadership and other processes of the organization must be such as to ensure a maximum probability that in all interactions and all relationships with the organization each member will, in the light of his background, values and expectations, view the experience as supportive and one which builds and maintains his personal worth and importance.

- **Chris Argyris**[3] who criticized formal organizations because they create in individuals 'feelings of failure and frustration, short time perspective and conflict'. To overcome this problem he advocated that individuals should have a high degree of self-control in setting their own goals and over defining the paths to these goals.
- **Frederick Herzberg**[4] who suggested that improvements in organization design must centre on the individual job as the positive source of motivation. If individuals feel the job is stretching them they will perform it well.
- **Abraham Maslow**[5] who emphasized that the higher order needs for self-fulfilment provide the greatest impetus to satisfaction and have to be catered for in job design processes.
- **Robert Blake**[6] who concentrated on management style – the way in which managers manage, based on their values and beliefs. He analyses management style against the two dimensions of 'concern for people' and 'concern for production'.
- **Warren Bennis**[7] who summarized OD beliefs as follows:

  — a new concept of humanity based on increased knowledge of their complex and shifting needs which replace an oversimplified, innocent, push-button idea of humanity;
  — a new concept of power, based on collaboration and reason, which replaces a model of power based on coercion and threat;
  — a new concept of organization values, based on humanistic–democratic ideas, which replaces the mechanistic value system of bureaucracy.

The organization development movement could be described as being heavily normative from the start: it provided a diagnosis and proposed solutions.

FEATURES OF ORGANIZATION DEVELOPMENT

Organization development programmes, as originally envisaged, were characterized by three main requirements.

1. They should be managed or at least strongly supported from the

top, but may make use of third parties or 'change agents' to diag-
nose problems and to manage change by means of various kinds
of planned 'interventions' in the organization's processes.
2. The plans for organization development should be based on a
systematic analysis and diagnosis of the organization, and the
change and problems facing it.
3. Behavioural science knowledge should be used to improve the
ways in which the organization copes in times of change, with
such processes as interaction, communication, participation,
planning and conflict.

ORGANIZATION DEVELOPMENT ACTIVITIES

The activities contained in a conventional 1970s type 'OD'
programme were typically as follows.

- **Implementing changed systems and structures** – taking into
account potential resistance to change and the need to ensure that
the people affected understand, accept and 'own' the change.
- **Integration** – improving the coordination of activities and the
way in which people cooperate with one another.
- **Team development** – improving the ways in which work groups
function.
- **Inter-group relations** – dealing with conflict situations between
work groups.
- **Educational activities** – developing skills, especially in the
processes of teamwork, interaction, problem solving, objective
setting and planning. These educational activities could be more
or less unstructured, as in laboratory or 'T group' training. Or
they could be built round a series of projects or workshops in
which participants are given scope to discover for themselves the
processes at work and to analyse the lessons they have learned. A
more structured approach is provided by the 'managerial grid'
programme of Blake and Mouton, which is based on an analysis
of management style.

MORE RECENT DEVELOPMENTS

The value of OD programming along the lines developed by the
pioneers was somewhat discredited in the 1980s. For example, in
1981 Adrian McLean[8] produced a damning critique of OD in which
he stated that

The theory of change and change management which is the foundation of most OD programmes is based on over-simplistic generalizations which offer little specific guidance to practitioners faced with the confusing complexity of a real change situation.... There seems to be a growing awareness of the inappropriateness of some of the value stances, models and prescriptions inherited from the 1960s.

The problem with OD was that practitioners often promised more than they could achieve. They tended to imply that the behavioural sciences provided all the answers, and that an integrated programme of 'intervention' would always significantly improve organizational health and effectiveness.

However, although it is right to dismiss programmed OD approaches as being irrelevant to the complex, indeed chaotic, 1990s, many of its concepts and the behavioural science theories upon which they were based have been incorporated into the currently favoured approaches to improving organizational effectiveness such as change management, team building and empowerment. And the diagnostic approach of the OD practitioners is still appropriate.

References

1. McGregor, D (1960) *The Human Side of Enterprise,* McGraw-Hill, New York.

2. Likert, R (1967) *The Human Organization*, McGraw-Hill, New York.

3. Argyris, C (1957) *Personality and Organization*, Harper & Row, New York.

4. Herzberg, F et al (1957) *The Motivation to Work,* Wiley, New York.

5. Maslow, A (1954) *Motivation and Personality*, Harper & Row, New York.

6. Blake, R et al (1964) 'Breakthrough in organizational development', *Harvard Business Review*, Vol 42.

7. Bennis, W (1960) *Organizational Development*, Addison-Wesley, Reading, Mass.

8. McLean, A (1981) 'Organization development: a case of the Emperor's New Clothes?', *Personnel Review*, Vol 1V, No 1.

ORGANIZATION DEVELOPMENT CHECKLIST

1. Is there any discrepancy between top management statements of values and their actual behaviour?

2. To what extent is communication laterally and vertically undistorted?
3. To what extent are people open and prepared to share all the relevant facts?
4. How much collaboration or competition is there between work groups?
5. Are win/lose activities characteristic of the relationships between individuals and groups?
6. Is constant attention given to redefining roles, relationships and organizational groupings in response to the changing nature of the organization's task, changes in the external environment and the changing needs of individual employees?
7. Is the right balance achieved between the demands of the task (the technical system) and the needs of individuals (the social system)?
8. To what extent can the climate in the organization be described as one of high suspicion or high trust?
9. What is the degree of mutual support in the organization? Is it a case of every person for him or herself or genuine concern for each other?
10. How is conflict handled:

   — on a win/lose basis; or
   — smoothed over without exploring the issues; or
   — by 'working through' the problem and reaching an integrated solution?

12. To what extent is control imposed from above or exercised by teams and people from within?
13. How far can the climate of the organization be described as:

   — restrictive with pressure for conformity, or
   — free and supportive with differences respected?

14. How well do people in the organization understand their objectives and roles?
15. How well do teams function in the sense of being cohesive, interdependent, making decisions by consensus and operating flexibly?

6

Managing organization culture

Corporate culture is the pattern of shared beliefs, attitudes, assumptions and values in an organization which may not have been articulated, but in the absence of direct instructions, shape the way people act and interact, and strongly influence the ways in which things get done.

This definition emphasizes that corporate culture refers to a number of abstractions (beliefs, attitudes etc) which pervade the organization although they may not have been defined in specific terms. Nevertheless, they can significantly influence people's behaviour and, therefore, the effectiveness of the organization. Programmes for improving organizational effectiveness must pay close attention to the existing culture. If this is impeding progress, ie is dysfunctional, then some action has to be taken to develop a more functional culture – one which will support the achievement of the organization's objectives. This is done through the process of culture management.

WHAT IS CULTURE MANAGEMENT?

Culture management is the process of developing or reinforcing an appropriate culture – that is, one which helps the organization to fulfil its purpose.

Culture management is concerned with the following.

■ Culture change, the development of attitudes, beliefs and values which will be congruent with the organization's mission, strategies, environment and technologies. The aim is to achieve significant changes in organizational climate, management style and behaviour which positively support the achievement of the organization's objectives.

■ Culture reinforcement, which aims to preserve and reinforce what is good or functional about the present culture.

■ Change management, which is concerned with enabling the culture to adapt successfully to change and gaining acceptance to changes in organization, systems, procedures and methods of work (see Chapter 7).

■ Commitment gain, which is concerned with the commitment of members of the organization to its mission, strategies and values (see Chapter 8).

Aims of culture management

The aims of culture management are to:

■ develop an ideology which guides management on the formulation and implementation of coherent strategies and policies for managing the organization and its members;

■ create and maintain a positive climate within an organization which indicates the behaviour which is expected of members of that organization in the course of their work;

■ promote understanding and commitment to the values of the organization.

Culture management does not, however, aim to impose a uniform and bland culture on an organization. It recognizes that different cultures may be appropriate in different parts of the firm. And, although there will be certain values which management believe are important, the process of disseminating these values will recognize that members of the organization will have their own sets of values which they will only modify if they are convinced that it is in their own interests as well as those of the organization.

The management of the organization's culture is a central activity for senior management with the advice and help of human resource management specialists in their increasingly important role as internal consultants.

Managements use strong culture to unite employees through a set of managerially sanctioned values. They set the direction and establish a culture which helps them to maintain it. Weak cultures are potentially more adaptable but will not be so effective in generating commitment to action.

The implication is that the pursuit of new strategic goals in response to environmental changes may require action to change the culture. However, changing strong cultures can be a prolonged affair, except in crisis conditions.

Culture management as a process should be based on an understanding of the significance and scope of corporate culture as discussed below.

SIGNIFICANCE AND SCOPE OF CORPORATE CULTURE

Corporate culture is a key component in the achievement of an organization's mission and strategies, the improvement of organizational effectiveness and the management of change.

The significance of culture arises because it is rooted in deeply held beliefs. It reflects what has worked in the past, being composed of responses which have been accepted because they have met with success.

Corporate culture can work for an organization by creating an environment which is conducive to performance improvement and the management of change. It can work against an organization by erecting barriers which prevent the attainment of corporate strategies. These barriers include resistance to change and lack of commitment.

The impact of culture can include:

■ conveying a sense of identity and unity of purpose to members of the organization;
■ facilitating the generating of commitment and 'mutuality';
■ shaping behaviour by providing guidance on what is expected.

Corporate culture can be described in terms of *values, norms and artefacts*. It will be perceived by members of the company as organizational climate and it will influence, and be influenced by, the organization's strategy, structure and systems.

Values

Values refer to what is regarded as important. They are expressed in beliefs on what is best or good for the organization and what sort of behaviour is desirable. The 'value set' of an organization may only be recognized at top level or it may be shared throughout the organization so that it could be described as being 'value driven'.

Clearly, the more strongly based the values, the more they will affect behaviour. This does not depend upon their having been articulated. Implicit values, which are deeply embedded in the culture of an organization and are reinforced by the behaviour of management, can be highly influential, while espoused values which are idealistic and are not reflected in managerial behaviour may have little or no effect.

Value areas in which values can be expressed might be:

- care and consideration for people;
- care for customers;
- competitiveness;
- enterprise;
- equity in the treatment of employees;
- excellence;
- growth;
- innovation;
- market/customer orientation;
- priority given to organizational rather than to people needs;
- performance orientation;
- productivity;
- provision of equal opportunity for employees;
- quality;
- social responsibility;
- teamwork.

Values are translated into reality through *norms* and *artefacts* as described below. They may also be expressed through the media of language (organizational jargon), rituals, stories and myths.

Norms

Norms are the unwritten rules of behaviour, the 'rules of the game' which provide informal guidelines on how to behave. Norms tell people what they are supposed to be doing, saying, believing, even wearing. They are never expressed in writing – if they were, they would be policies or procedures. They are passed on by word of mouth or behaviour and can be enforced by the reactions of people if they are violated. They can exert very powerful pressure on behaviour because of these reactions – we control others by the way we react to them.

Norms refer to aspects of behaviour like these.

- How managers treat subordinates and how subordinates relate to their subordinates.
- The prevailing work ethic, eg 'Word hard, play hard', 'Come in early, stay late', 'If you cannot finish your work during business

hours you are obviously inefficient', 'Look busy at all times', 'Look relaxed at all times'.

■ Status – how much importance is attached to it; the existence or lack of obvious status symbols.

■ Ambitions – naked ambition is expected and approved of, or a more subtle approach is the norm.

■ Performance – exacting performance standards are general; the highest praise that can be given in the organization is to be referred to as being very professional.

■ Power – recognized as a way of life; executed by political means, dependent on expertise and ability rather than position; concentrated at the top; shared at different levels in different parts of the organization.

■ Politics – rife throughout the organization and treated as normal behaviour; not accepted as overt behaviour.

■ Loyalty – expected, a cradle to grave approach to careers; discounted, the emphasis is on results and contribution in the short term.

■ Anger – openly expressed; hidden, but expressed through other, possibly political, means.

■ Approachability – managers are expected to be approachable and visible; everything happens behind closed doors.

■ Formality – a cool, formal approach is the norm; forenames are/are not used at all levels; there are unwritten but clearly understood rules about dress.

Artefacts

Artefacts are the visible and tangible aspects of an organization which people hear, see or feel. Artefacts can include such things as the working environment, the tone and language used in letters or memorandums, the manner in which people address each other at meetings or over the telephone, and the welcome (or lack of welcome) given to visitors and the way in which telephonists deal with outside calls. Artefacts can be very revealing.

Organizational climate

Organizational climate is less encompassing than the concept of organizational culture and is more readily measured by such means as attitude surveys. Organizational climate is how people perceive (see and feel about) the culture that has been created in their company or unit.

Management style

Management style describes the way in which managers set about achieving results through people. It is how managers behave as team leaders and how they exercise authority. Managers can be autocratic or democratic, tough or soft, demanding or easy-going, directive or *laissez-faire*, distant or accessible, destructive or supportive, task orientated or people orientated, rigid or flexible, considerate or unfeeling, friendly or cold, keyed up or relaxed. How they behave will depend partly on themselves and their natural inclinations, partly on the example given to them by their managers, and partly on organizational values and norms.

Culture and strategy

Strategic choices on such matters as growth, innovation, product-market development and human resource development will shape behaviour, and, progressively, change values and norms. But the culture of the organization could equally help to shape its strategy. For example, a company with an open, enterprising and flexible culture is more likely to adopt this approach when developing its business strategies. Culture and strategy are interdependent.

Culture and process

Process is broadly 'the way things are done around here'. It embraces such aspects of organizational behaviour as leading, motivating, gaining commitment, managing change, working with others, and planning and coordinating activities. Policies, procedures, structures and systems are means of making process work.

Culture management will involve influencing behaviour, attitudes and beliefs through process. For example, total quality as a concept can be developed through various quality control mechanisms but will only be fully achieved if processes in the organization fully support its achievement.

Culture and structures or systems

Corporate culture will affect the ways in which the organization is structured and its operational systems. These will include the amount of rigidity or flexibility allowed in the structure, the extent to which networking and other informal processes of interaction and communication override or replace formal channels, empowerment, the amount of authority which is devolved from the top or the centre, and the degree to which jobs are compartmentalized and rigidly defined. It may affect the number of layers of management, the spans of control of managers and the extent to which decisions are made by teams rather than by individuals.

The development and use of systems will also be affected by the corporate culture, and will in turn help to shape it. A bureaucratic or mechanistic organization will attempt to govern everything through systems or manuals. A more flexible or organic approach will only allow systems which can be changed easily in response to new demands, and are functions of the situation in which the enterprise finds itself rather than conforming to any predetermined and rigid view of how it should operate. In some organizations, people follow systems to the letter, while in others, people take pride in 'bucking the system' and cutting corners to get things done. Systems can be used as control mechanisms to enforce conformity or they can be flexed to allow scope for adapting to new situations as they arise.

Development of culture

The norms and values which are the basis of culture will be developed over time as a result of the influence of the organization's external environment, and its internal processes, systems and technology.

The external environment covers economic, market, competitive and social trends, technological innovations, and government interventions. Internally, culture is shaped by the purpose, strategy and technology of the organization, and by particularly significant events, such as a major crisis or the impact of a dynamic, visionary and inspirational chief executive. In fact, the philosophy and values of top management over the years will have played a dominant role.

Varieties of culture

The strength of a culture will clearly influence its impact on corporate behaviour. Strong cultures will have more widely shared, and more clearly expressed beliefs and values. These values will probably have been developed over a considerable period of time and they will be perceived as functional in the sense that they help the organization to get things done.

There have been attempts to develop typologies of cultures, such as the work of Charles Handy[1]. And cultures can sometimes be described in one phrase such as 'command culture' where management imposes its will on employees or a 'culture of consent' which operates more democratically. But such descriptions tend to be superficial.

There may be one culture pervading the organization, but there will almost certainly be a number of subcultures in different departments, functions or divisions. This can complicate culture management because of possible inconsistencies or conflicts between cultures.

In fact, an important question to answer when considering cultural change is the extent to which a common culture should be developed (or imposed) throughout the organization or the degree to which strategic business units should continue to maintain their own distinctive cultures. The answer to this question will depend on the philosophy of top management, which in turn will affect and be affected by the nature of the organization and its operation.

Culture may also be strongly influenced by different product-market conditions or different technologies. In Book Club Associates, for example, the culture in its London office, where business was generated through marketing and advertising activities, was flexible, innovative and informal. This was quite different from the culture in its Swindon operational division, which was essentially a paper factory and was therefore much more disciplined, rigid and formal.

The more operational responsibility is devolved the less pressure there will be from the centre to adopt a common culture on the basis that what matters is 'what you achieve rather than how you achieve it'.

Implications

Culture is developed and manifests itself in different ways in different organizations. It is not possible to say that one culture is better than another, only that it is dissimilar in certain ways. There is no such thing as an ideal culture, only an appropriate culture. This means that there can be no universal prescription for managing culture, although there are certain approaches which can be helpful, as described in the next section.

APPROACHES TO CULTURE MANAGEMENT

Culture management is about reinforcing or embedding an existing functional culture, or changing a dysfunctional culture. The approach will be affected by certain overall considerations as discussed below. With these in mind, culture management is a matter of analysis and diagnosis followed by the application of appropriate reinforcement or change levers.

Overall considerations

Ed Schein[2] has suggested that the most powerful primary mechanisms for culture embedding and reinforcement are:

- what leaders pay attention to – what they measure and control;
- leaders' reactions to critical incidence and crises;
- deliberate role modelling, teaching and coaching by leaders;
- the criteria for allocation of rewards and status;
- the criteria for recruitment, selection, promotion and commitment.

Because cultures have evolved over the years and are usually deeply rooted, they are difficult to change. It is very hard to get people to alter long-held attitudes and beliefs, and attempts to do so often fail. All you can do is to get them to alter their behaviour in ways which will reduce dysfunctional elements in the culture and support the introduction of functional elements.

But changing behaviour is not always easy, although it will happen in traumatic circumstances such as a crisis, a change in ownership or the arrival of a powerful, autocratic, charismatic and visionary leader.

Analysis and diagnosis

The analysis of culture and the diagnosis of what management action needs to be taken can be carried out on a continuous basis by observation, and noting behaviours which indicate the values and norms prevalent in the organization.

A more searching analysis would use instruments such as interviews, questionnaires, focus groups (representative groups of employees whose views are sought on organizational or work issues), attitude surveys and workshops.

Culture management programmes

One or more of the following approaches can be used to help in managing culture.

- The issue of mission and value statements which explicitly state where the organization is going and the values it adopts in getting there – but these statements must represent reality and must be followed up by workshops, training and discussions which translate the words into deeds.

■ Workshops to get people involved in discussing new values and ways of behaviour, and practising their application.

■ Education and training programmes to extend knowledge and teach people new skills.

■ Performance management programmes which ensure through the mechanisms of objective setting, defining competence requirements and performance appraisal that the values, norms and behaviours which the cultural change programme is developing are absorbed and acted upon as part of the normal process of management.

■ Reward management systems which reward people for behaviour which is in accord with the values built into the culture change programme.

Such programmes can be used not only to change but also to reinforce a culture. Ideally, they are should be conducted on an organization-wide basis, but it may have to be recognized that different parts of the organization can legitimately have different cultures and that it could be counter-productive to impose an alien culture upon them.

Individual managers can make a vital contribution by first understanding their culture, secondly by getting involved as far as possible in the definition of the aims and constituents of a culture management programme, and, finally, playing their part by practising the required behaviour themselves, developing it in their staff and instilling or reinforcing the value system of the organization throughout their department.

References

1 Handy. C (1981) *Understanding Organizations,* Penguin Books, Harmondsworth.

2. Schein, E (1987) *Organization Culture and Leadership,* Jossey Bass, New York.

CULTURE MANAGEMENT CHECKLIST

1. Has the mission of the organization been defined and communicated to all concerned?

2. What are the norms of the organization (i.e. how people behave or are expected to behave) under such headings as:

   — the work ethic;
   — status;
   — ambition;
   — performance;
   — exercise of power;
   — playing politics;
   — managerial behaviour;
   — formality/informality;
   — openness;
   — trust;
   — interpersonal relations?

3. What are the core values of the organization and staff (ie what is believed to be important) under such headings as:

   — balance between needs of organization and staff;
   — care and consideration for people;
   — care for customers and clients;
   — competitiveness;
   — cost control;
   — enterprise;
   — equity in the treatment of staff;
   — excellence;
   — flexibility;
   — growth;
   — innovation;
   — market/customer orientation;
   — performance orientation;
   — provision of opportunity for employees;
   — quality;
   — social responsibility?

4. To what extent have these values been defined and communicated to employees?
5. What action has been taken by management to ensure that the values have been put into practice?

6. To what extent can the climate of the organization (its working atmosphere) be described as:

   — action oriented;
   — bureaucratic;
   — cooperative;
   — formal;
   — friendly;
   — hierarchical;
   — innovative;
   — open (communicative);
   — people oriented;
   — political;
   — proactive;
   — reactive;
   — relaxed;
   — results oriented;
   — status conscious;
   — stressful;
   — task oriented?

7. What do employees feel about:

   — the degree of formality or informality in the working atmosphere;
   — how well they are trusted to carry out important work;
   — the sense of riskiness and challenge in the job and in the organization – the relative emphasis on taking calculated risks or playing it safe;
   — the existence of friendly and informal social groups;
   — the perceived helpfulness of managers and co-workers – the emphasis (or lack of emphasis) on mutual support;
   — the perceived importance of implicit and explicit goals and performance standards, the emphasis on doing a good job, the challenge represented in personal and team goals;
   — the extent to which management is willing to listen to different opinions;

— the degree of emphasis on getting problems out into the open, rather than smoothing them over or ignoring them;
— that they belong to the organization – that they are valuable members of a working team;
— the organization as such – the extent to which they are committed to its goals and performance standards?

8. To what extent are managers:

— autocratic, ie using authority to compel people to do what they are told, or democratic, ie encouraging people to participate in decision making;
— task-centred or people-centred;
— distant and cold or approachable and friendly;
— hard or soft on people?

9. To what extent, and in what ways, are the norms, values, climate and management style of the organization functional or dysfunctional, ie how far do they support or inhibit the achievement of objectives?

10. How receptive is top management to any need for cultural change?

7

Change management

Change is the only thing that remains constant in organizations. Effective organizations take deliberate steps to manage change smoothly. They will not always succeed – change can be a traumatic process – but at least they will try.

The approach to the management of change will recognize that the key to success lies not only in a transformational leader supported by powerful change mechanisms, but also by understanding that change is implemented by people, and that it is their behaviour and support that count. The most important aim of change management is to achieve commitment to change.

Successful change management requires an understanding of:

■ the main types of change;
■ how change affects individuals;
■ the process of change;
■ how to build commitment to change.

TYPES OF CHANGE

There are two main types of change: strategic and operational.

Strategic change

Strategic change is concerned with broad, long-term and organization-wide issues. It is about moving to a future state which has been defined generally in terms of strategic vision and scope. It will cover the purpose and mission of the organization, its corporate philosophy on such matters as growth, quality, innovation and values concerning people, the customer needs served and the technologies employed.

This overall definition leads to specifications of competitive positioning, and strategic goals for achieving and maintaining competitive advantage and for product-market development. These goals are supported by policies concerning marketing, sales, manufacturing, product and process development, finance and human resource management.

Strategic change takes place within the context of the external competitive, economic and social environment, and the organization's internal resources, capabilities, culture, structure and systems. Its successful implementation requires thorough analysis and understanding of these factors in the formulation and planning stages. The ultimate achievement of sustainable competitive advantage relies on the two qualities defined by Andrew Pettigrew and Richard Whipp[1]:

> The capacity of the firm to identify and understand the competitive forces in play and how they change over time, linked to the competence of a business to mobilize and manage the resources necessary for the chosen competitive response through time.

Strategic change, however, should not be treated simplistically as a linear process of getting from A to B which can be planned and executed as a logical sequence of events. The research conducted by Pettigrew and Whipp into competitiveness and managing change in the motor, financial services, insurance and publishing industries led them to observe that:

> The process by which strategic changes are made seldom move directly through neat, successive stages of analysis, choice and implementation.

Operational change

Operational change relates to new systems, procedures, structures or technology which will have an immediate effect on working arrangements within a part of the organization. But their impact on people can be more significant than broader strategic change and they have to be handled just as carefully.

HOW PEOPLE CHANGE

The ways in which people change are best explained by reference to the following assumptions developed by Bandura[2]:

- people make conscious choices about their behaviours;

■ the information people use to make their choices comes from their environment;

■ their choices are based upon
— the things that are important to them
— the views they have about their own abilities to behave in certain ways
— the consequences they think will accrue to whatever behaviour they decide to engage in.

For those concerned with change management, the implications of this theory are that the tighter the link between a particular behaviour and a particular outcome, the more likely it is that we will engage in that behaviour, and the more desirable the outcome, the more likely it is that we will engage in behaviour that we believe will lead to it. Furthermore, the more confident we are that we can actually assume a new behaviour, the more likely we are to try it.

To change people's behaviour, therefore, we have first to change the environment within which they work, secondly, to convince them that the new behaviour is something they can accomplish (training is important) and, thirdly, to persuade them that it will lead to an outcome they will value. None of these steps is easy. To achieve them, it helps to know more about the process of change.

THE PROCESS OF CHANGE

Change, as Rosabeth Moss Kanter[3] puts it, is the process of analysing 'the past to elicit the present actions required for the future'. It involves moving from a present state, through a transition state to a future desired state.

The process starts with an awareness of the need for change. An analysis of this state and the factors that have created it leads to a diagnosis of the distinctive characteristics of the situation, and an indication of the direction in which action needs to be taken. Possible courses of action can then be identified and evaluated, and a choice made of the preferred action.

It is then necessary to decide how to get from here to there. Managing the process of change is a critical phase in this state of transition. It is here that the problems of introducing change emerge and have to be managed. These problems can include resistance to change, low stability, high levels of stress, misdirected energy, conflict and losing momentum. Hence the need to do everything possible to anticipate reactions and likely impediments to the introduction of change.

The installation stage can also be painful. When planning change there is a tendency for people to think that it will be an entirely logical and linear process of going from A to B. It is not like that at all. As described by Pettigrew and Whipp[1], the implementation of change is an 'iterative, cumulative and reformulation-in-use process'.

THE APPROACH TO CHANGE MANAGEMENT

Michael Beer and his colleagues suggested in a seminal *Harvard Business Review* article 'Why change programs don't produce change'[4], that most such programmes are guided by a theory of change which is fundamentally flawed. This theory states that changes in attitudes lead to changes in behaviour: 'According to this model, change is like a conversion experience. Once people "get religion", changes in their behaviour will surely follow.'

They believe that this theory gets the change process exactly backwards:

> In fact, individual behaviour is powerfully shaped by the organizational roles people play. The most effective way to change behaviour, therefore, is to put people into a new organizational context, which imposes new roles, responsibilities and relationships on them.

They prescribe six steps to effective change which concentrate on what they call 'task alignment' – reorganizing employees' roles, responsibilities and relationships to solve specific business problems in small units where goals and tasks can be clearly defined. The aim of following the overlapping steps is to build a self-reinforcing cycle of commitment, coordination and competence. The steps are as follows.

1. Mobilize commitment to change through the joint analysis of problems.
2. Develop a shared vision of how to organize and manage to achieve goals such as competitiveness.
3. Foster consensus for the new vision, competence to enact it and cohesion to move it along.
4. Spread revitalization to all departments without pushing it from the top – don't force the issue, let each department find its own way to the new organization.
5. Institutionalize revitalization through formal policies, systems

6. Monitor and adjust strategies in response to problems in the revitalization process.

The approaches suggested by Michael Beer and his colleagues is fundamental to the effective management of change. They can be associated with a number of other guidelines as set out below.

GUIDELINES FOR CHANGE MANAGEMENT

- The achievement of sustainable change requires strong commitment and leadership from the top.
- Understanding is necessary of the culture of the organization and the levers for change which are most likely to be effective in that culture.
- Those concerned with managing change at all levels should have the temperament and leadership skills appropriate to the circumstances of the organization and its change strategies.
- It is important to build a working environment which is conducive to change. This means developing the firm as a 'learning organization' (see Chapter 16).
- Although there may be an overall strategy for change, it is best tackled incrementally (except in crisis conditions). The change programme should be broken down into actionable segments for which people can be held accountable.
- The reward system should encourage innovation and recognize success in achieving change.
- Change implies streams of activity across time and 'may require the enduring of abortive efforts or the build up of slow incremental phases of adjustment which then allow short bursts of incremental action to take place' (Pettigrew and Whipp[1]).
- Change will always involve failure as well as success. The failures must be expected and learned from.
- Hard evidence and data on the need for change are the most powerful tools for its achievement, but establishing the need for change is easier than deciding how to satisfy it.
- It is easier to change behaviour by changing process, structure and systems than to change attitudes or the corporate culture.
- There are always people in organizations who welcome the challenges and opportunities that change can provide. They are the ones to be chosen as change agents.
- Resistance to change is inevitable if the individuals concerned feel that they are going to be worse off – implicitly or explicitly.

The inept management of change will produce that reaction.

■ In an age of global competition, technological innovation, turbulence, discontinuity, even chaos, change is inevitable and necessary. The organization must do all it can to explain why change is essential and how it will affect everyone. Moreover, every effort must be made to protect the interests of those affected by change.

GAINING COMMITMENT TO CHANGE

These guidelines point in one direction: having decided why changes are necessary, what the goals are and how they are to be achieved, the most important task is to gain the commitment of all concerned to the proposed change.

A strategy for gaining commitment to change should cover the following phases.

1. **Preparation**   In this phase, the person or persons likely to be affected by the proposed change are contacted in order to be made aware of the fact that a change is being contemplated.
2. **Acceptance**   In the second phase, information is provided on the purpose of the change, how it is proposed to implement it and what effect it will have on those concerned. The aim is to achieve understanding of what the change means and to obtain a positive reaction. This is more likely if:

   — the change is perceived to be consistent with the mission and values of the organization;
   — the change is not thought to be threatening;
   — the change seems likely to meet the needs of those concerned;
   — there is a compelling and fully understood reason for change;
   — those concerned are involved in planning and implementing the change programme on the principle that people support what they help to create;
   — it is understood that steps will be taken to mitigate any detrimental effects of the change.

   It may be difficult, even impossible, to meet these requirements. That is why the problems of gaining commitment to change should not be underestimated.

   During this phase, the extent to which reactions are positive or negative can be noted and action taken accordingly. The original plans may have to be modified to cater for legitimate reservations or second thoughts.

3. **Commitment** During the third phase, the change is implemented and becomes operational. The change process and people's reaction to it need to be monitored. There will inevitably be delays, setbacks, unforeseen problems and negative reactions from those faced with the reality of change. A response to these reactions is essential so that valid criticisms can be acted upon or explanations given of why it is believed that the change should proceed as planned.

Following implementation, the aim is to get the change adopted as, with use, its worth becomes evident. The decision is made at this stage on whether to continue with the change, or whether it needs to be modified or even aborted. Account should again be taken of the views of those involved.

Finally, and after further modifications as required, the change is institutionalized, and becomes an inherent part of the organization's culture and operations.

References

1. Pettigrew, A and Whipp, R (1991) *Managing Change for Competitive Success*, Blackwell, Oxford.

2. Bandura, A (1986) *Social Boundaries of Thought and Action*, Prentice-Hall, Englewood Cliffs, NJ.

3. Kanter, R M (1984) *The Change Masters*, Allen & Unwin, London.

4. Beer, M, Eisenstat, R and Spector, B (1990) 'Why change programs don't produce change', *Harvard Business Review 1990*, November–December.

CHANGE MANAGEMENT CHECKLIST

Top management

1. Is there a deep consensus among the top team about the context the business is in and what needs to be done to achieve sustainable good performance?
2. Is there an understanding of the change strategy the organization should pursue now and how this may alter over time?

3. Is there a deep and broad 'feel' for the organization – how it works, what it is like, what needs to be changed, and what should be preserved and sustained?

4. Is there an understanding of the appropriate 'levers' for change (actions, processes, interventions, communications) which can be used to direct and manage a change process?

5. Are there people in leadership positions who are suited by temperament and skills to the particular change strategy being pursued?

Establishing the need for change

6. Have the problems that necessitate change been properly diagnosed?

7. Are goals set which define the future state or organizational conditions desired after the change?

8. Have the transition state activities, and commitments required to meet the future state, been defined?

9. Have strategies and action plans been developed for managing the transition?

Developing change strategies

10. Has a climate been built up within the organization which will make people in general receptive to change? (This involves justifying why change should take place.)

11. Has the organization the capacity to plan the change before attempting to introduce it?

12. Has a change agenda been established which not only sets the direction in which the organization is going, but also establishes the necessary visions and values?

13. Are planned changes an integral part of overall corporate strategies?

Planning the implementation of change

14. Have steps been taken to mobilize commitment to change through the joint analysis of organizational problems?

15. Have intentions been broken down into actionable components?
16. Have managers or teams who can act as change agents been identified ?
17. Has responsibility for the actionable components been allocated to change managers who can act in small or easily defined units to solve specific problems for which goals and tasks can be clearly defined?
18. In planning change, is there full awareness that, except in crisis conditions, an incremental approach often works best?
19. In planning change, have steps been taken to ensure that relevant information, appropriate resources and expert support is available to those involved in the change process?
20. Is full account taken in planning change of how people will be affected by it, what their reactions are likely to be, how it can be managed to satisfy individual as well as organizational needs (as far as possible), and how the need for change can be presented in a way which is fully understood and provides compelling reasons for the change?
21. Are people involved in planning change aware of the fact that a working compromise is better than an optimal solution, poorly implemented?
22. Is there a full awareness of the fact that it is easier to change behaviour by changing processes, structure or systems, than to change attitudes or the corporate culture?

Gaining commitment to change

23. Are proper steps taken to ensure that those likely to be affected by change are informed that a change is being contemplated, and why?
24. In presenting the reason for change, are determined efforts made to achieve understanding of what the change means and to obtain a positive reaction?
25. As far as is possible, are steps taken to reduce the threatening aspects of proposed changes?
26. Are as many people as possible involved in planning and implementing the change programme in order to maximize 'ownership' of the change?

Implementing change

27. Are adequate steps taken to monitor the implementation of change?
28. Is everyone realistic about the likelihood that there will be delays, setbacks, unforeseen problems and negative reactions from those faced with the reality of change?
29. Are those concerned with managing change therefore prepared to respond to negative reactions and criticism either to modify the planned change or to spell out why the change should go ahead as planned?
30. Is it recognized that a 'grand design' for comprehensive change may have to be modified in practice and the change implemented in incremental steps?
31. When the change has been introduced, are steps being taken to institutionalize it through articulated policies, procedures and systems?

8

Leadership

Leaders have a key role to play in developing effective organizations. They set people in the right direction and motivate them to achieve goals by satisfying their needs and by stressing the value of their contribution. They recognize and reward success, which not only gives people a sense of accomplishment, but also helps them to feel that they belong to an organization which cares for them.

As John Kotter[1] has written:

> The direction-setting aspect of leadership does not produce plans; it creates visions and strategies. These describe a business, technology or corporate culture in terms of what it should become over the long term and articulate a feasible way of achieving this goal.

WHAT IS LEADERSHIP?

Leadership is getting things done through people. It happens when there is an objective to be achieved, or a task to be carried out, and when more than one person is needed to do it. All managers, are by definition, leaders in that they can only do what they have to do with the support of their team, who must be inspired or persuaded to follow them. Leadership is therefore about encouraging and inspiring individuals and teams to give of their best to achieve a desired result.

The overall aim of leaders is to achieve the task with the help of their group. To meet this overall aim leaders have three main objectives.

1. To gain the commitment and cooperation of their team.
2. To get the group into action to achieve agreed objectives.
3. To make the best use of the skills, energies and talents of the team.

Leaders aim to get people to do what they think is necessary by obtaining willing cooperation, not grudging submission. They build up the morale of their groups, which will be high when the group is productive and works well together. The members of the group do not need to be made comfortable; in fact, they will often be under pressure to do more than they would if left to their own devices. But if they achieve something worth while together they will gain satisfaction from that.

LEADERSHIP QUALITIES

Effective leaders focus on a fairly small range of key issues, have a very clear idea of what they want to do about those issues, and have the ability to set the direction and take people with them.

Successful leadership sometimes seems to depend on having the right qualities at the right time. But what are the factors that influence and develop these qualities? A study of chief executives in the UK produced the following ranked list of influences on success:

		Rating out of 100
1.	Ability to work with people	78
2.	Early responsibility for important tasks	75
3.	A need to achieve results	75
4.	Leadership experiences early in career	74
5.	Wide experience in many functions	68
6.	Ability to do deals and negotiate	66
7.	Willingness to take risks	63
8.	Ability to have better ideas than colleagues	62
9.	Having talents 'stretched' by immediate bosses	60
10.	Ability to change managerial style to suit occasion	58

This list is a mix of abilities or skills (1, 3, 6, 7, 8 and 10) and the types of experience which have developed those abilities (2, 4, 5 and 9). It highlights the fact that natural abilities are only part of the picture. They are nurtured by experience, and the situations in which potential and existing leaders have found themselves.

Leadership is largely an acquired skill. To start with, a leader needs intelligence, a positive attitude and a combination of the qualities of courage, shrewdness and common sense. Successful leaders, as they gain experience, build on these natural talents and develop the wide range of skills they need.

PERSONALITY TRAITS OF SUCCESSFUL LEADERS

While it may not be possible to be definite about the abilities or skills that unequivocally characterize effective leaders in all situations, there is good evidence that there are certain basic personality traits which tend to characterize leaders in a wide variety of situations. In general, leaders are more intelligent than their followers, although not too much so, lest they appear to be remote, with difficulties in communicating and getting their views accepted. Leaders also tend to be better adjusted, more dominant, more extrovert, less conservative, and to have a better understanding of people than the rank and file. It is interesting to note that these characteristics are sometimes latent, only emerging when people are put into leadership positions.

TYPES OF LEADERS

Leaders can be defined in terms of characteristics, success factors and personality traits. To answer the question 'Who is a leader?' it is also helpful to explore how these combine to produce different types of leaders.

Leadership types can be classified in a number of ways and the following are some of the most typical categorizations.

1. **Charismatic/non-charismatic**   Charismatic leaders rely on their aura, their personality and their inspirational qualities. These are natural characteristics, although experience may have taught them how best to project themselves. Non-charismatic leaders rely mainly on their know-how, their ability to give an impression of quiet confidence and their cool, analytical approach to dealing with problems.
2. **Autocratic/democratic**   Autocratic leaders impose their decisions and tend to surround themselves with yes-people. They use their position to force people to do what they are told. Democratic leaders encourage people to participate and involve themselves in decision taking. They will exert their authority to get things done but will rely more on know-how and persuasive ability than the use of position power.

3. **The visionary/enabler or the controller/manipulator** The visionary/enabler inspires people with their vision of the future. The controller/manipulator is concerned mainly with operating the internal system.
4. **Transactional or transformational** Burns[2] distinguishes between transactional leaders who exchange money, jobs and security for compliance, and transformational leaders who motivate others to strive for higher order goals rather than merely short-term interest.

THE ROLE OF THE LEADER

Leaders have two essential roles, as follows.

1. **Achieve the task** – that is why their group exists. The leader's role is to ensure that the group's purpose is fulfilled. If it is not, the result is frustration, disharmony, criticism and, eventually perhaps, disintegration of the group.
2. **Maintain effective relationships** – between themselves and the members of the group, and within the group. These relationships are effective if they are conducive to achieving the task. They can be divided into those concerned with the team and its morale and sense of common purpose, and those concerned with individuals and how they are motivated.

John Adair[3] has suggested that these demands are best expressed as three areas of need which leaders are there to satisfy. These are:

1. **task needs** – to get the job done;
2. **group needs** – to build up and maintain team spirit;
3. **individual needs** – to harmonize the needs of the individual with the needs of the task and the group.

These three needs are interdependent and are best expressed as three overlapping circles (see Figure 8.1).

THE LAW OF THE SITUATION

The type of leadership exercised and success as a leader depends to a large extent on the situation and the leader's ability to understand it and act accordingly. The situation comprises the nature of the task, the impact of the organization – its policies, culture and environment,

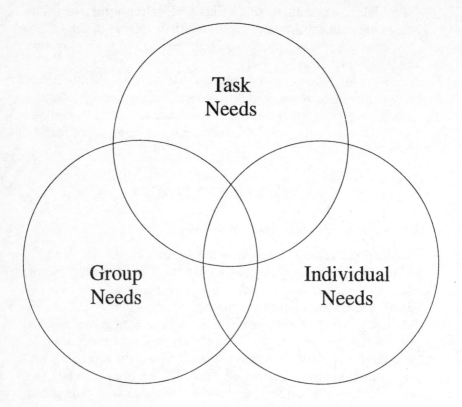

Figure 8.1 Leadership needs

the degree to which the situation is structured or ambiguous, the sort of people in the working group and the type of authority the leader has – given or assumed.

The performance of a group, as Fiedler[4] pointed out, is related to both the leadership style and the degree to which the situation provides the leader with the opportunity to exert influence. His research indicated that a task-oriented approach worked best for leaders in situations which are highly favourable. In the very favourable conditions when the leader has power, formal backing and a relatively well-structured task, the group is ready to be directed and told what to do.

In unfavourable conditions such as an emergency, the task-oriented leader will be more effective than the considerate leader who is concerned with interpersonal relationships. The latter will do better in a somewhat unstructured or ambiguous situation, or where his or her power as a leader is restricted

Fiedler called this his contingency theory of leadership and emphasized the situational aspects of being a leader:

> Leadership performance then depends as much on the organization as on the leader's own attributes. Except perhaps for the unusual case, it is simply not meaningful to speak of an effective leader or an ineffective leader, we can only speak of a leader who tends to be effective in one situation and ineffective in another.

Not only does the situation affect the type of leadership required, but it will also create conditions under which new and different types of leaders will emerge who are appropriately qualified to meet changing demands.

References

1. Kotter, J (1980) 'What leaders really do', *Harvard Business Review*, May-June.
2. Burns, J (1978) *Leadership*, Harper & Row, New York.
3. Adair, J (1984) *Action Centred Leadership*, McGraw-Hill, London.
4. Fiedler, F A (1967) *Theory of Leadership Effectiveness*, McGraw-Hill, New York.

LEADERSHIP CHECKLIST

The task

1. What needs to be done and why?
2. What results have to be achieved?
3. What problems have to be overcome?
4. Is the solution to these problems straightforward or is there a measure of ambiguity?
5. Is this a crisis situation?
6. What is the time-scale for completing the task?
7. What pressures are going to be exerted on the leader?

The team

8. What is the composition of the team?
9. How well is the team organized?

10. Do the members of the team work well together?
11. What will they want to get out of this?
12. How can the commitment of this particular team be achieved?
13. How are results to be obtained by satisfying their needs?
14. How are they likely to respond to the various leadership styles or approaches which may be adopted?

The in   dividuals in the team

15. What are the strengths and weaknesses of each member of the team?
16. What sort of things are likely to motivate them?
17. How are they likely to respond individually to the various leadership techniques or styles the leader may adopt?

9

Motivating

Organizational effectiveness depends on people who are motivated to give of their best. The organization as a whole, and its individual managers and team leaders, have the responsibility for providing the context and the processes which will maximize the degree to which people are motivated.

To do this it is necessary to understand:

■ the process of motivation;
■ the different types of motivation;
■ the basic concepts of motivation;
■ the implications of motivation theory;
■ applications of motivation;
■ the roles of financial and non-financial rewards as motivators.

THE PROCESS OF MOTIVATION

Motivation is concerned with goal-directed behaviour. People are motivated to do something if they think it will be worth their while.

The process of motivation is initiated by someone recognizing an unsatisfied need. A goal is then established which, it is thought, will satisfy the need, and a course of action is determined which is expected to lead towards the attainment of the goal.

Basically, therefore, management and managers motivate people by providing means for them to satisfy their unsatisfied needs. This can be done by offering incentives and rewards for achievement and effort. But the needs of individuals and the goals associated with them vary so widely that it is difficult, if not impossible, to predict precisely how a particular incentive or reward will affect individual behaviour.

Motivation can also be achieved through the work itself by means of job design. The social context will also affect the level of motivation. This context will consist of the organization culture generally, management style (the way in which individuals are managed) and the influence of the group or team in which the individual works.

TYPES OF MOTIVATION

Motivation at work can take place in two ways. First, people can motivate themselves by seeking, finding and carrying out work which satisfies their needs or at least leads them to expect that their goals will be achieved. Secondly, people can be motivated by management through such methods as pay, promotion, praise etc.

These two types of motivation are described in the following way.

- **Intrinsic motivation**   the self-generated factors which influence people to behave in a particular way or to move in a particular direction. These factors include responsibility (feeling the work is important and having control over one's own resources), freedom to act, scope to use and develop skills and abilities, interesting and challenging work and opportunities for advancement.
- **Extrinsic motivation**   what is done to or for people to motivate them. This includes rewards such as increased pay, praise or promotion; and punishments, such as disciplinary action, withholding pay or criticism.

The extrinsic motivators can have an immediate and powerful effect, but this will not necessarily last for long. The intrinsic motivators, which are concerned with the quality of working life, are likely to have a deeper and longer term effect because they are inherent in individuals and not imposed from outside.

BASIC CONCEPTS OF MOTIVATION

The basic concepts of motivation are concerned with needs, goals, reinforcement and expectations (expectancy theory).

Needs

Needs theory states that behaviour is motivated by unsatisfied needs. The key needs associated with work are those for achievement, recognition, responsibility, influence and personal growth.

Goals

Goal theory states that motivation will be increased if goal-setting techniques are used with the following characteristics:

- the goals should be specific;
- they should be challenging but reachable;
- the goals should be seen as fair and reasonable;
- individuals participate fully in goal-setting;
- feedback ensures that people get a feeling of pride and satisfaction from the experience of achieving a challenging but fair goal;
- feedback is used to gain commitment to even higher goals.

Reinforcement

Reinforcement theory suggests that successes in achieving goals and rewards act as positive incentives and reinforce the successful behaviour, which is repeated the next time a similar need arises.

Expectancy theory

Expectancy theory states that for there to be a heightened motivation to perform, individuals have to:

- feel able to change their behaviour;
- feel confident that a change in their behaviour will produce a reward;
- value the reward sufficiently to justify the change in behaviour.

Expectancy theory applies just as much to non-financial as to financial rewards. For example, if people want personal growth they will only be motivated by the opportunities available to them if they know what these opportunities are, if they know what they need to do to benefit from them (and can do it) and if the opportunities are worth striving for.

Expectancy theory explains why extrinsic motivation – for example, an incentive or bonus scheme – works only if the link between effort and reward is clear, and the value of the reward is worth the effort. It also explains why intrinsic motivation arising from the work itself can sometimes be more powerful than extrinsic motivation. Intrinsic motivation outcomes are more under the control of individuals, who can place greater reliance on their past experiences to indicate the extent to which positive and advantageous results are likely to be obtained by their behaviour.

IMPLICATIONS OF MOTIVATION THEORY

Motivation theory conveys two important messages. First, there are no simplistic solutions to increasing motivation. No single lever such as performance-related pay exists which is guaranteed to act as an effective motivator. This is because motivation is a complex process. It depends on:

- **individual needs and aspirations** which are almost infinitely variable;
- both **intrinsic and extrinsic motivating factors** and it is impossible to generalize on what the best mix of these is likely to be;
- **expectations** about rewards which will vary greatly among individuals according to their previous experiences and perceptions of the reward system;
- **the social context** where the influences of corporate culture, managers and co-workers can produce a wide variety of motivational forces which are difficult to predict and therefore to manage.

The second key message provided by motivation theory is the significance of expectations, goal-setting, feedback and reinforcement as motivating factors.

The implications of these messages are considered below.

APPROACHES TO MOTIVATION

Creating the right climate

It is necessary in general to create a climate which will enable high motivation to flourish. This is a matter of managing the organization culture. The aims would be, first, to reinforce values concerning performance and competence; second, to emphasize norms (accepted ways of behaviour) relating to the ways in which people are managed and rewarded; and third, to demonstrate the organization's belief in empowerment – providing people with the scope and 'space' to exercise responsibility and use their abilities to the full (see also Chapter 11). Without the right climate, quick fixes designed to improve motivation such as performance-related pay are unlikely to make much of an impact on overall organizational effectiveness, although they may work with some individuals.

Job design

Job design, as described in Chapter 4, can provide intrinsic motivation by satisfying the needs of individuals for interest, challenge and accomplishment.

Recognizing complexity

Motivation policies should recognize the complexity of the motivation process and not attempt to adopt simplistic solutions to motivational problems. The organization should provide for a mix of various types of intrinsic and extrinsic motivation and make use of both financial and non-financial incentives. But it should be borne in mind that the social context and the ways in which these incentives are managed for individuals will be key factors influencing their effectiveness.

Goal-setting, feedback and reinforcement

Provision should be made for goal-setting, feedback and reinforcement to be major features of the management and reward processes. Performance management processes as discussed in Chapters 17 can fulfil this purpose well.

Managing expectations

It is necessary to manage expectations. No reward offered through an incentive, bonus or performance-related pay scheme will be effective as a motivator unless individuals believe it is worth while and can reasonably expect to obtain it through their own efforts.

The implications of these approaches as they affect financial and non-financial reward policies and practices are discussed below.

FINANCIAL REWARDS

Financial rewards need to be considered from three points of view:

- the effectiveness of money as a motivator;
- the reasons why people are satisfied or dissatisfied with their rewards;
- the criteria which should be used when developing a financial reward system.

Money and motivation

Money is important to people because it is instrumental in satisfying a number of their most pressing needs. It is significant not only because of what they can buy with it, but also as a highly tangible method of recognizing their worth, thus improving their self-esteem and gaining the esteem of others.

Pay is the key to attracting people to join an organization, although job interest, career opportunities and the reputation of the organization will also be factors. Satisfaction with pay among existing employees is mainly related to feelings about equity and fairness. External and internal comparisons will form the basis of these feelings, which will influence their desire to stay with the organization.

Pay can motivate. As a tangible means of recognizing achievement, pay can reinforce desirable behaviour. Pay can also deliver messages on what the organization believes to be important. But, to be effective, a pay-for-performance system has to meet the following stringent conditions:

- there must be a clear link between performance and reward;
- the methods used to measure performance should be perceived to be fair and consistent;
- the reward should be worth striving for;
- individuals should expect to receive a worthwhile reward if they behave appropriately.

NON-FINANCIAL REWARDS

Non-financial rewards can be focused on the needs most people have, although to different degrees, for achievement, recognition, responsibility, influence and personal growth.

Achievement

The need for achievement is defined as the need for competitive success measured against a personal standard of excellence.

Achievement motivation can be increased by organizations through processes such as job design, performance management and skill or competency–based pay schemes.

Recognition

Recognition is one of the most powerful motivators. People need to know not only how well they have achieved their objectives or carried out their work but also that their achievements are appreciated.

Praise, however, should be given judiciously – it must be related to real achievements. And it is not the only form of recognition. Financial rewards, especially achievement bonuses awarded immediately after the event, are clearly symbols of recognition to which are attached tangible benefits, and this is an important way in which mutually reinforcing processes of financial and non-financial rewards can operate. And there are other forms of recognition such as long-service awards, status symbols of one kind or another, sabbaticals and trips abroad, all of which can be part of the total reward process.

Recognition is also provided by managers who listen to and act upon the suggestions of their team members and, importantly, acknowledge their contribution. Other actions which provide recognition include promotion, allocation to a high-profile project, enlargement of the job to provide scope for more interesting and rewarding work, and various forms of status or esteem symbols.

The recognition processes in an organization can be integrated with financial rewards through performance management and pay-for-performance schemes. The importance of recognition can be defined as a key part of the value set of the organization and this would be reinforced by education, training and performance appraisals.

Responsibility

People can be motivated by being given more responsibility for their own work. This is essentially what empowerment, as discussed in Chapter 11, is about and is in line with the concept of intrinsic moti-

vation based on the content of the job. It is also related to the fundamental concept that individuals are motivated when they are
provided with the means to achieve their goals.

The characteristics required in jobs if they are to be intrinsically
motivating are that first, individuals must receive meaningful feedback about their performance, preferably by evaluating their own
performance and defining the feedback they require, second, the job
must be perceived by individuals as requiring them to use abilities
they value in order to perform the job effectively, and third, individuals must feel that they have a high degree of self-control over setting
their own goals and over defining the paths to these goals.

Providing motivation through increased responsibility is a matter
of job design and the use of performance management processes.

Influence

People can be motivated by the drive to exert influence or to exercise
power. David McClelland's[1] research established that along with the
need for achievement, the need for power was a prime motivating
force for managers, although the need for 'affiliation', ie warm,
friendly relationships with others, was always present. The organization, through its policies for involvement, can provide motivation by
putting people into situations where their views can be expressed,
listened to and acted upon. This is another aspect of empowerment.

Personal growth

In Maslow's[2] hierarchy of needs, self-fulfilment or self-actualization
is the highest need of all and is therefore the ultimate motivator. He
defines self-fulfilment as 'the need to develop potentialities and
skills, to become what one believes one is capable of becoming'.

Ambitious and determined people will seek and find these opportunities for themselves, although the organization needs to clarify the
scope for growth and development it can provide (if it does not, they
will go away and grow elsewhere).

Increasingly, however, individuals at all levels of organizations,
whether or not they are eaten up by ambition, recognize the importance of upgrading their skills continually and of developing their
careers progressively. Many people now regard access to training as
a key element in the overall reward package. The availability of

learning opportunities, the selection of individuals for high-prestige training courses and programmes, and the emphasis placed by the organization on the acquisition of new skills as well as the enhancement of existing ones, can all act as powerful motivators.

References

1. McClelland, D (1975) *Power, The Inner Experience*, Irvington, New York.
2. Maslow, A (1954) *Motivation and Personality*, Harper & Row, New York.

MOTIVATION CHECKLIST

To what extent have the following approaches to motivation been adopted?

1. Set and agree demanding goals.
2. Provide feedback on performance.
3. Create expectations that certain behaviours and outputs will produce worthwhile rewards when people succeed but will result in penalties if they fail.
4. Design jobs which enable people to feel a sense of accomplishment, to express and use their abilities and to exercise their own decision-making powers.
5. Provide appropriate financial incentives and rewards for achievement (pay-for-performance).
6. Provide appropriate non-financial rewards such as recognition and praise for work well done.
7. Communicate to individuals and publicize generally the link between performance and reward – thus enhancing expectations.
8. Select and train managers and team leaders who will exercise effective leadership and have the required motivating skills.
9. Give people guidance and training which will develop the knowledge, skills and competences they need to improve their performance.
10. Show individuals what they have to do to develop their careers.

10

Gaining commitment

THE MEANING OF ORGANIZATIONAL COMMITMENT

Commitment is about attachment and loyalty. It refers to the relative strength of an individual's identification with, and involvement in, a particular organization. It consists of three factors:

1. a strong desire to remain a member of the organization;
2. a strong belief in, and acceptance of, the values and goals of the organization;
3. a readiness to exert considerable effort on behalf of the organization.

THE SIGNIFICANCE OF COMMITMENT

There have been two schools of thought about commitment. One, the 'from control to commitment' school, was led by Richard Walton[1], who saw commitment strategy as a more rewarding approach to human resource management, in contrast to the traditional control strategy. The other, 'Japanese/excellence' school, is represented by writers such as Pascale and Athos, and Peters (see Chapter 1), who looked at the Japanese model and related the achievement of excellence to getting the wholehearted commitment of the workforce to the organization.

From control to commitment

The importance of commitment was highlighted by Richard Walton. His theme was that improved performance would result if the organization moved away from the traditional control-oriented approach to workforce management, which relies upon establishing order, exercising control and 'achieving efficiency in the application of the workforce'. He argued that this approach should be replaced by a commitment strategy. He suggested that workers respond best – and most creatively – not when they are tightly controlled by management, placed in narrowly defined jobs and treated like an unwelcome necessity, but, instead, when they are given broader responsibilities, encouraged to contribute and helped to achieve satisfaction in their work.

Walton suggested that in the new commitment-based approach:

> Jobs are designed to be broader than before, to combine planning and implementation, and to include efforts to upgrade operations, not just to maintain them. Individual responsibilities are expected to change as conditions change, and teams, not individuals, often are the organizational units accountable for performance. With management hierarchies relatively flat and differences in status minimized, control and lateral coordination depend on shared goals. And expertise rather than formal position determines influence.

The Japanese/excellence school

Attempts made to explain the secret of Japanese business success by a number of writers led to the theory that the best way to motivate people is to get their full commitment to the values of the organization by leadership and involvement. This might be called the 'hearts and minds' approach to commitment and, among other things, it popularized such devices as quality circles.

The baton was taken up by Peters and Waterman[2] and their imitators later in the 1980s. This approach to excellence was summed up by Peters and Austin[3] when they wrote:

> Trust people and treat them like adults, enthuse them by lively and imaginative leadership, develop and demonstrate an obsession for quality, make them feel they own the business, and your workforce will respond with total commitment.

Commitment and motivation

In relating commitment to motivation it is useful to distinguish, as do Buchanan and Huczynski[4], three perspectives.

1. The goals towards which people aim. From this perspective, goals such as the good of the company or effective performance at work may provide a degree of motivation for some employees, who could be regarded as committed in so far as they feel they own the goals.
2. The process by which goals and objectives at work are selected, which is quite distinct from the way that commitment arises within individuals.
3. The social process of motivating others to perform effectively. From this viewpoint, strategies aimed at increasing motivation also affect commitment. It may be true to say that, where commitment is present, motivation is likely to be strong, particularly if a long-term view is taken of effective performance.

Commitment and organizational effectiveness

Strong commitment to work will contribute to organizational effectiveness because it is likely to result in conscientious and self-directed application to do the job, regular attendance, nominal supervision and a high level of effort. Commitment to the organization will certainly be related to the intention to stay – in other words, loyalty to the company.

CREATING COMMITMENT

Steps to create commitment can include communication, education and training programmes, initiatives to increase involvement and 'ownership', and the development of performance and reward management systems.

Communication programmes

It seems to be strikingly obvious that commitment will only be gained if people understand what they are expected to commit to. But managements too often fail to pay sufficient attention to delivering the message in terms which recognize that the frame of reference for those who receive it is likely to be quite different from their own. Management's expectations will not necessarily coincide with those of employees. And, in delivering the message, the use of different and complementary channels of communication such as newsletters, briefing groups, videos, notice boards etc is often neglected.

Part of the communication process is to share the values of management with employees and encourage them to uphold those values. But it should be remembered that this *is* a sharing process. Values cannot be forced down people's throats. People will only accept them if they are congruent with their own values. The process of getting values acted upon can be a long-term one which involves the use of educational, training and performance management processes as well as communications. And none of these will work if employees perceive that management is not behaving in accordance with its espoused values, either in the way the organization is run or how employees are treated.

It is also desirable for management to avoid defining and communicating values in such a way as to inhibit flexibility, creativity and the ability to adapt to change. Strategies have to be defined in broad terms with caveats that they will be amended if circumstances change. Values have to emphasize the need for flexibility, innovation and teamworking, as well as the need for performance and quality.

Education

Education is another form of communication. An educational programme is designed to increase both knowledge and understanding of, for example, total quality management. The aim will be to influence behaviour and thereby progressively change attitudes.

Training

Training is designed to develop specific skills and competences. For example, if one of the values to be supported is flexibility, it will be necessary to extend the range of skills possessed by members of work teams through multiskilling programmes.

Commitment is enhanced if managers can gain the confidence and respect of their teams, and training to improve the quality of management should form an important part of any programme for increasing commitment. Management training can also be focused on increasing the competence of managers in specific areas of their responsibility for gaining commitment, eg performance management.

Developing ownership

A sense of belonging is enhanced if there is a feeling of 'ownership' among employees; not just in the literal sense of owning shares (although this can help), but in the sense of believing they are genuinely accepted by management as a key part of the organization. This concept of 'ownership' extends to participating in decisions on new developments and changes in working practices which affect the individuals concerned. They should be involved in making those decisions and feel that their ideas have been listened to, and that they have contributed to the outcome. They will then be more likely to accept the decision or change because it is owned by them rather than being imposed by management. The concept of ownership is closely linked to that of empowerment as discussed in Chapter 11.

Developing a sense of excitement in the job

A sense of excitement in the job can be created by concentrating on the intrinsic motivating factors such as responsibility, achievement and recognition, and using these principles to govern the way in which jobs are designed. Excitement in the job is also created by the quality of leadership, and the willingness of managers and supervisors to recognize that they will obtain increased motivation and commitment if they pay continuous attention to the ways in which they delegate responsibility, and give their staff the scope to use their skills and abilities.

Performance management

A performance management system is based on agreements between managers and individuals on objectives, standards of performance and improvement plans. Performance is then managed and reviewed against these objectives.

This system can help to cascade corporate objectives and values throughout the organization so that consistency is achieved at all levels. Discussions on individual objectives are carried out within the context of departmental, unit and, ultimately, organizational objectives. The expectations of individuals are thus defined in terms of their own job, which they can more readily grasp and act upon than if they were asked to support some remote and, to them, irrelevant overall objectives. But individual objectives can be described in ways which support the achievement of those defined for higher levels in the organization.

Reward management

Reward management systems can make it clear that individuals will be rewarded in accordance with the extent to which they achieve objectives *and* uphold corporate values. The reward system can thus be used to reinforce the messages delivered through other channels of communication.

CONCLUSIONS

Too much should not be expected from campaigns to increase commitment. They may reduce labour turnover, increase identification with the organization and develop feelings of loyalty among its employees. They may increase job satisfaction, but there is no evidence that higher levels of job satisfaction necessarily improve performance. They may provide a context within which motivation and therefore performance levels will increase. But there is no guarantee that this will take place, although the chances of gaining improvements will be increased if the campaign is focused upon a specific value such as quality.

It may be naïve to believe that 'hearts and minds' campaigns to win commitment will transform organizational behaviour overnight. But it is surely important for organizations to do what they can along the lines described above to influence behaviour, to support the achievement of objectives and to uphold values that are inherently worthwhile. It is good management practice to define the organization's expectations in terms of objectives and standards of performance. It is even better management practice to discuss and agree these objectives and standards with employees.

References

1. Walton, R (1985) 'From control to commitment', *Harvard Business Review*, March–April.
2. Peters, T and Waterman, R (1982) *In Search of Excellence*, Harper & Row, New York.

3. Peters, T and Austin, N (1985) *A Passion for Excellence*, Collins, Glasgow.

4. Buchanan, D and Huczynski, A (1985) *Organizational Behaviour*, Prentice-Hall, Englewood Cliffs, NJ.

COMMITMENT CHECKLIST

To what extent have the following steps been taken to increase commitment?

1. Define and disseminate the mission and values of the organization.
2. Develop shared objectives by ensuring that everyone understands the strategies of the organization and participates in setting his or her own objectives within the framework of those strategies.
3. Get people involved in defining problems and working out solutions in order that they 'own' any changes emerging from this process.
4. Provide transformational leadership from the top which can inspire people with a vision for the future.
5. Use every medium of communication available to get messages across about the organization's mission, values, strategies and objectives.
6. Ensure by example and training that the prevailing management style in the organization encourages involvement and teamwork.
7. Develop processes and an organizational climate which encourage people's growth in terms of skill and greater competence.
8. Introduce organization-wide profit or gainsharing plans which encourage people to identify with the organization.
9. Use induction training programmes to ensure that new employees form a good impression of the organization from the outset.
10. Use workshops and other forms of training to get people together to discuss the issues affecting the organization, and to give them the opportunity to contribute their own ideas. Take action on good ideas that emerge from these discussions.

11

Empowerment

WHAT IS EMPOWERMENT?

Empowerment is the process of giving people more scope or 'power' to exercise control over, and take responsibility for, their work.

Empowerment provides greater 'space' for individuals to use their abilities by enabling and encouraging them to take decisions close to the point of impact.

BASIS

The basis for the belief that empowerment is a valid approach to improving organizational effectiveness is that people who are nearest to the problem are best able to judge its solution, provided they have a framework within which to make their decisions.

Assumptions about the empowered organization

Charles Handy[1] has suggested that these are the assumptions behind the concepts of the empowered organization.

- **Competence** the belief that individual employees can be expected to perform to the limit of their competence with the minimum of supervision.
- **Trust**   it is necessary not only to believe in people's competence but also to trust them to get on with the job.
- **Teamwork**   few organizational problems can be solved by one person acting alone. The sheer rate of change and turbulence means that as new challenges and problems appear, people must naturally group together in flexible teams without barriers of status or hierarchy, to solve the problems within the framework of the organization's goals and values. The organization is held

together by these beliefs and values – by people who are committed to one another and to their common goals.

Reasons for empowerment

The reasons for empowerment are that it:

- can speed up decision-making processes and reaction times;
- releases the creative and innovative capacities of employees;
- provides for greater job satisfaction, motivation and commitment;
- gives people more responsibility;
- enables employees to gain a greater sense of achievement from their work;
- reduces operational costs by eliminating unnecessary layers of management, staff functions, and quality control and checking operations.

Replacing the command organization

A 'command' organization is one in which decision making is centralized, reliance is placed on the authority of managers to 'get things done', management believes it always knows best, however far away it is from the scene of action (the client or the customer) and the contributions of staff are taken for granted rather than welcomed.

In contrast, the empowered organization makes much better use of the ability and enthusiasm of its employees. It has the potential to improve continuously by a series of small and large steps day after day, and at all levels, feeding back the learning from its experience to make it work better. In the words of Tom Peters[2] it replaces 'control by procedure with control by vision and trust'.

The command organization can be likened to a dinosaur with its tiny brain impotently issuing instructions to its massive body, while the empowered organization is more like a shoal of fish, moving rapidly and consistently, and adjusting through instantly understood signals.

THE PROCESS OF EMPOWERMENT

Empowerment can be achieved through:

- structural means – organizational and work grouping;
- the behaviour or style of individual managers;
- enlisting the support of employees in tackling immediate organizational issues;

■ gaining the 'hearts and minds' of people.

Structural empowerment – organizational

An empowered organization is likely to have a flat structure with the minimum number of management layers. A multilayered structure filters the two-way flow of information and hinders decision making from penetrating as far down the organization as it should.

Structural empowerment – work group

As suggested by Christian Schumacher[3] of *Small is Beautiful* fame, empowerment can be achieved at the work group level by applying the following principles.

1. Work should be organized around basic operations to form 'whole tasks'.
2. The basic organizational unit should be the primary workgroup (ie 4–20 people).
3. Each workgroup should include a designated leader.
4. Each workgroup and its leader should, as far as possible, plan and organize its own work.
5. Each workgroup should be able fully to evaluate its performance against agreed standards of excellence.
6. Jobs should be structured so that workgroup members can personally plan, execute and evaluate at least one operation in the process.
7. All workgroup members should have the opportunity to participate in the group's processes of planning, problem solving and evaluation.

Management style

Managers empower the members of their teams, not by giving up control but by changing the way control is exercised. They have to learn to delegate more, and to allow individuals and teams more scope to plan, act and monitor their own performance.

But they still have the responsibility to provide guidance and support to their staff as required. They must also help them to develop the skills and competences they need to function effectively in an empowered organization.

Involvement in issues

Empowerment can be achieved by involving people in developing their own solutions to specific issues. This can be done by expecting teams not simply to propose ways forward or to hope that someone else will do something, but actually to solve the problem in their part of the organization, in accordance with the resources they have and the constraints within which they work.

At General Electric, the Chief Executive, Jack Welch[4], arranged for employees at all levels in the organization to get together and work out how the ways in which things got done could be improved. His aim was 'to give people a voice, give them a say, give them a chance to participate'. In describing these 'work outs' he also said that:

> Ultimately, we're talking about redefining the relationship between boss and subordinate. I want to get to the point where people challenge their bosses every day: 'Why do you require me to do wasteful things? Why don't you let me do things you shouldn't be doing so you can move on and create? That's the job of the leader – to create, not to control. Trust me to do my job and don't make me waste all my time trying to deal with you on control issues.'

Hearts and minds

Empowerment is about engaging both the hearts and minds of people so that they can take the opportunities made available to them for increased responsibility.

At management level this is achieved by sharing strategic vision and corporate values throughout the organization, creating the assumption of competence and furthering the trust without which an empowered organization cannot operate.

References

1. Handy, Charles (1990) *The Age of Unreason*, Arrow Books, London.
2. Peters, T (1988) *Thriving on Chaos*, Macmillan, London.
3. Schumacher, Christian (1976/77) 'Structuring work', *Industrial Participation*, Winter.
4. Welch, Jack (1991) quoted in *Managing People and Organizations*, J Gabarro (ed), Harvard Business School Publications, Boston, Mass.

EMPOWERMENT CHECKLIST

1. Do managers generally understand the concept of empowerment, and how it can help to improve the organization's and their own effectiveness?

2. To what extent is this a 'command' organization, relying on managerial authority to get things done or an 'empowered' organization in which people are generally given more scope to exercise control over, and take responsibility for, their work?

3. To what extent have groups of employees been empowered in the sense that they have been given a say in how their work should be organized and in solving work problems?

4. Is the climate generally one of belief in the competence of employees and a feeling of trust that, with appropriate training and support, they will get on with the job?

5. Are there so many management layers in the organization and so much checking at each level that decision making close to the point of action is seriously hindered?

6. Are jobs structured so that individuals can plan, execute and evaluate a complete operation in the total process personally ?

7. Are managers actually delegating more and allowing individuals and teams greater scope to plan, act and monitor their own performance?

8. Are teams and individuals encouraged to develop their own solutions to specific issues?

9. Do managers provide the support, guidance and training required to ensure that empowered teams and individuals can operate effectively?

10. Does the reward system recognize achievements on the part of managers in empowering their staff and on the part of individuals in making a bigger contribution in a climate of empowerment?

12

Teamworking

THE SIGNIFICANCE OF TEAMWORKING

Organizational effectiveness is largely about making the best use of people. Although human resource management policies and practices often focus on the individual, it has to be recognized that organizations are cooperative systems which consist of groups of people working together. They may be working in formal groups set up to achieve a defined purpose or they may be working informally.

Teamworking becomes more significant when the technology or operating processes require 'cellular' working or considerable interaction between people carrying out different functions but with a common purpose. Effective teamworking is more important during periods of rapid change or crisis. An organization which has to adapt quickly to its changing competitive, economic or social environment will rely upon good teamwork, so that it can pool resources and respond fast to the new opportunities or threats.

The top management team in a responsive and adaptive organization will often operate on a collegiate basis. Each director may be concerned with a particular function or discipline, but they share responsibility for results, and get involved jointly and severally to deal with issues. Informal subgroups or task forces are created when necessary which cut across functional boundaries and address a common task. The leader of the top management team – the chief executive officer – will join in the task forces on equal terms. Leadership may indeed be assumed by any member of the team who has the special skills required to deal with the situation.

The tendency for organizations to become flatter as layers of management or supervision are stripped out creates the need for better teamwork. In these circumstances managers will have larger spans of control and will have to delegate more responsibility to their teams, who will be forced to coordinate their own work rather than rely upon their boss to do it for them. In this type of organization inter-disciplinary project teams become more important. The instant availability of management information and the communication facilities provided by information technology assist informal teams to operate more efficiently.

At office or shop floor level autonomous workgroups may be set up which are responsible for all aspects of their operation and may not be closely controlled by a designated supervisor.

Organizations need to develop approaches and policies which promote effective teamwork in the situations described above. This chapter examines how such policies can be developed and applied under the following headings.

- What is a team?
- Team processes.
- Team development.
- Team effectiveness.
- Team roles.
- Approach to achieving good teamwork.
- Teamworking in action.
- Introducing teamworking.
- Teambuilding and interactive skills training.

WHAT IS A TEAM?

As defined by Katzenbach and Smith[1]:

> A team is a small number of people with complementary skills who are committed to a common purpose, performance goals and approach for which they hold themselves mutually accountable.

They suggested that the some of the main characteristics of teams are as follows.

- Teams are the basic units of performance for most organizations. They meld together the skills, experiences and insights of several people.
- Teamwork applies to the whole organization as well as specific teams. It represents 'a set of values that encourage behaviours such as listening and responding cooperatively to points of view expressed by others, giving others the benefit of the doubt,

providing support to those who need it, and recognizing the interests and achievements of others.'

■ Teams are created and energized by significant and demanding performance challenges.

■ Teams outperform individuals acting alone or in large organizational groupings, especially when performance requires multiple skills, judgements and experiences.

■ Teams are flexible and responsive to changing events and demands. They can adjust their approach to new information and challenges with greater speed, accuracy and effectiveness than can individuals caught in the web of larger organizational connections.

■ High-performance teams invest much time and effort exploring, shaping and agreeing on a purpose that belongs to them, both collectively and individually. They are characterized by a deep sense of commitment to their growth and success.

TEAM EFFECTIVENESS

An effective team is likely to be one in which the structure, leadership and methods of operation are relevant to the requirements of the task. There will be commitment to the whole group task, and people will have been grouped together in a way which ensures that they are related to each other by way of the requirements of task performance and task interdependence.

In an effective team its purpose is clear and its members feel the task is important, both to them and to the organization. According to Douglas McGregor[2] the main features of a well-functioning, creative team are as follows.

1. The atmosphere tends to be informal, comfortable and relaxed.
2. There is a lot of discussion in which initially everyone participates, but it remains pertinent to the task of the group.
3. The task or objective of the team is well understood and accepted by the members. There will have been free discussion of the objective at some point, until it was formulated in such a way that the members of the team could commit themselves to it.
4. The members listen to each other. Every idea is given a hearing. People do not appear to be afraid of being considered foolish by putting forth a creative thought even if it seems fairly extreme.

5. There is disagreement. Disagreements are not suppressed or overridden by premature team action. The reasons are carefully examined and the team seeks to resolve them rather than to dominate the dissenter.
6. Most decisions are reached by consensus in which it is clear that everybody is in general agreement and willing to go along. Formal voting is at a minimum; the team does not accept a simple majority as a proper basis for action.
7. Criticism is frequent, frank and relatively comfortable. There is little evidence of personal attack, either openly or in a hidden fashion.
8. People are free in expressing their feelings as well as their ideas both on the problem and on the group's operation.
9. When action is taken, clear assignments are made and accepted.
10. The leader of the team does not dominate it, nor does the team defer unduly to the leader. There is little evidence of a struggle for power as the team operates. The issue is not who controls, but how to get the job done.

These characteristics together present an ideal which might be striven for but is seldom attained. The extent to which it is possible or even desirable for them to be achieved depends on the situation. A mechanistic or bureaucratic type of enterprise – where this is appropriate to the technology – cannot allow its formal organizational units to function just like this, although it should try to ensure that any committees, task forces or project teams which are set up do exhibit these forms of behaviour.

Richard Walton[3] has commented that in the new commitment-based organization it will often be teams rather than individuals who will be the organizational units accountable for performance.

However, teamwork, as Peter Wickens[4] has said, 'is not dependent on people working in groups but upon everyone working towards the same objectives'. The Nissan concept of teamwork, as quoted by Wickens, is expressed in its General Principles and emphasizes the need to:

■ promote mutual trust and cooperation between the company, its employees and the union;
■ recognize that all employees, at whatever level, have a valued part to play in the success of the company;
■ seek actively the contributions of all employees in furthering these goals.

Waterman[5] has noted that teamwork 'is a tricky business; it requires people to pull together toward a set of shared goals or values. It does not mean that they always agree on the best way to get there. When they don't agree they should discuss, even argue these differences'.

Richard Pascale[6] underlined this point when he wrote that successful companies can use conflict to stay ahead: 'We are almost always better served when conflict is surfaced and channelled, not suppressed.' The pursuit of teamwork should not lead to a 'bland' climate in the organization in which nothing new or challenging ever happens. It is all very well to be 'one big happy family', but this could be disastrous if it breeds complacency and a cosy feeling that the family spirit comes first, whatever is happening in the outside world.

TEAMBUILDING AND INTERACTIVE SKILLS DEVELOPMENT

Teambuilding training aims to:

- increase awareness of the social processes which take place within groups;
- develop the interactive or interpersonal skills which enable individuals to function effectively as team members;
- increase the overall effectiveness with which groups operate in the organization.

To be effective, teambuilding and other interpersonal development programmes should be directly relevant to the responsibilities of the participants and be seen as relevant by participants, their managers, subordinates and colleagues. They need to support business objectives, fit in with practical working arrangements and reflect the values the organization wishes to promote.

TEAM MANAGEMENT

Team management is the process of ensuring that teams work effectively in accordance with the criteria set out above.

To achieve this aim, the role of team managers or leaders is to clarify purpose and goals, build commitment and self-confidence, strengthen the team's collective skills and approach, remove externally imposed obstacles, and create opportunities for team members to develop their skills and competences.

References

1. Katzenbach, J and Smith, D (1993) *The Magic of Teams*, Harvard Business School Press, Boston, Mass.

2. McGregor, D (1960) *The Human Side of Enterprise*, McGraw-Hill, New York.

3. Walton, R (1985) 'From control to commitment', *Harvard Business Review*, March–April.

4. Wickens, P (1987) *The Road to Nissan*, Macmillan, London.

5. Waterman, R (1988) *The Renewal Factor*, Bantam, New York.

6. Pascale, R (1990) *Managing on the Edge*, Viking, London.

CHECKLIST OF THINGS TO DO TO ACHIEVE GOOD TEAMWORK

1. Establish urgency and direction.
2. Select members based on skills and skill potential, not personalities. They should be good at working with others but still capable of taking their own line when necessary.
3. Pay particular attention to first meetings and actions.
4. Set immediate performance-oriented tasks and goals.
5. Set overlapping or interlocking objectives for people who have to work together. These will take the form of targets to be achieved or projects to be completed by joint action.
6. Assess people's performance, not only on the results they achieve, but also on the degree to which they are good team members. Recognize and reward people who have worked well in teams (using team bonus schemes where appropriate), bearing in mind that being part of a high-performance team can be a reward in itself.
7. Encourage people to build networks – things get done in organizations, as in the outside world, on the basis of whom you know as well as what you know.
8. Set up interdepartmental project teams with a brief to get on with it.

to get on with it.

9. Describe and think of the organization as a system of interlocking teams united by a common purpose. Don't emphasize hierarchies. Abolish departmental boundaries if they are getting in the way, but do not be alarmed if there is disagreement – remember the value of *constructive* conflict.

10. Hold special 'off-the-job' meetings for work teams so they can get together and explore issues without the pressures of their day-to-day jobs.

11. Use training programmes to build relationships. This can often be a far more beneficial result of a course than the increase in skills or knowledge which was its ostensible purpose.

12. Use teambuilding and interactive skills training to supplement the other approaches. But do not rely upon them to have any effect unless the messages they convey are in line with the organization's culture and values.

13
Flexibility

THE NEED FOR FLEXIBILITY

There are four good reasons why an effective organization today has to operate flexibly:

1. **The need to be competitive** This focuses attention on the more efficient use of human resources.
2. **The need to be adaptive** The organization has to be able to respond quickly to change and to the new demands constantly being made upon it in turbulent and highly competitive conditions.
3. **The impact of new technology** This is changing skill requirements and working arrangements – for example, cellular manufacturing systems.
4. **New organization structures** The emergence of what Henry Mintzberg termed the 'adhocracy' – a more fluid form of organization in which complex innovation takes place – requires a more flexible approach to structure, the definition of work roles and how roles interact.

Although competitive pressures and new technologies may generally indicate that greater structural and operating flexibility is required, the extent to which this applies in any one organization must depend entirely on its environment and its technology. A bureaucratic and inflexible approach might be appropriate in some circumstances; a much more flexible approach might be unavoidable in others. And there will always be a choice – depending on the situation – of what priorities should be given to the different types of flexibility.

FUNCTIONAL, NUMERICAL AND FINANCIAL FLEXIBILITY

It was suggested by Atkinson[1] that there are three kinds of flexibility:

1. **Functional flexibility** which is sought so that employees can be redeployed quickly and smoothly between activities and tasks. Functional flexibility may require *multiskilling* – craft workers who possess and can apply a number of skills covering, for example, both mechanical and electrical engineering, or manufacturing and maintenance activities.
2. **Numerical flexibility** which is sought so that the number of employees can be quickly and easily increased or decreased in line with even short-term changes in the level of demand for labour.
3. **Financial flexibility** which provides for pay levels to reflect the state of supply and demand in the external labour market, and also means the use of flexible pay systems which facilitate either functional or numerical flexibility.

THE FLEXIBLE FIRM

It was also claimed by Atkinson that there is a growing trend for firms to seek all three kinds of flexibility by developing an entirely new organization structure. This results in the development of what he termed the 'flexible firm'.

The new structure in the flexible firm involves the break-up of the labour force into increasingly peripheral, and therefore numerically flexible, groups of workers clustered around a numerically stable core group which will conduct the organization's key, firm-specific activities. At the core, the emphasis is on functional flexibility. Shifting to the periphery, numerical flexibility becomes more important. As the market grows, the periphery expands to take up slack; as growth slows, the periphery contracts. At the core, only tasks and responsibilities change; the workers here are insulated from medium-term fluctuations in the market, whereas those in the periphery are exposed to them.

FLEXIBILITY ARRANGEMENTS

Flexibility arrangements as means of achieving increased organizational effectiveness can take the following forms:

- **contract-based** new forms of employment contracts;
- **time-based** shift working and flexible hours;
- **job-based** job-related flexibilities;
- **skills-based** multiskilling;
- **organization-based** the use of contract workers and part-timers;
- **pay-based** more flexible reward systems.

Contract-based flexibility

Contract-based flexibility refers to employee contracts which specify flexibility as a key aspect of terms and conditions. Job descriptions are written in terms which emphasize the overall purpose of the job and its principal accountabilities. These are broadly related to the achievement of corporate or departmental objectives. The job description does not specify in detail the duties to be carried out by the job holder and may contain a catch-all phrase such as 'accountable for the performance of such other duties as are required to achieve the overall purpose of the job'. Contract-based flexibility is also achieved by employing contract workers who are required to work on any task or in any area appropriate to their range of skills.

Time-based flexibility

Time-based flexibility can be achieved by the use of flexible hours. The most familiar method is flexitime in which employees can vary their daily hours of work on either side of the core time when they have to be present, providing the longer term required hours are completed. Time flexibility can be achieved in companies with marked seasonal fluctuations in labour requirements, such as photo processing, by negotiating annual hours agreements. These specify the annual hours to be worked and paid for, but within that total they incorporate provisions for longer hours at peak periods and shorter hours during troughs.

Job-based flexibility (functional flexibility)

Job-based flexibility means that workers can be moved from task to task and may be expected to use a wider range of skills within their capability. Firms may want to introduce this type of flexibility because they need to make the fullest use of their human resources, especially when they are using increasingly sophisticated equipment and systems which must be properly maintained if they are to produce at their optimum level. Functional flexibility also means that where work loads in different parts of a factory fluctuate widely, people can be moved in quickly to handle the extra demands.

In the UK, the 1970s and 1980s saw the end of many of the old demarcation rules which had bedevilled flexibility in British industry. A typical union agreement (Nissan Motor) stipulated the following.

1. To ensure the fullest use of facilities and manpower, there will be complete flexibility and mobility of employees.
2. It is agreed that changes in technology, processes and practices will be introduced, and that such changes will affect both productivity and manning levels.
3. To ensure such flexibility and change, employees will undertake training for all work as required by the company. All employees will train other employees as required.

These arrangements are fairly typical, especially in international firms setting up in green-field sites. Full functional flexibility is often associated with integrated pay schemes, and the harmonization of terms and conditions of employment so that all staff, both office and factory workers, are covered by the same pay structure and are treated alike as far as benefits are concerned.

Skill-based flexibility (multiskilling)

Functional flexibility is only possible when employees have the range of skills required to perform different tasks, for example machine operators having the necessary skills not only to operate their machinery, but also to carry out basic maintenance and deal with minor faults and breakdowns.

At Hardy Spicer, a form of 'just-in-time' manufacture was introduced which included an integrated flexible flow line of dedicated CNC (computer numerical control) machine cells, linked by a robotized pallet convey or system and programmable controls. This type of manufacturing system pointed to the need for multiskilling in which 'system technicians' on the production line had to have a range of skills including machine set up and basic maintenance, as well as taking responsibility for loading, quality and output. These technicians had to have a wide understanding of tool gauging, hydraulics, electrics and basic electronics. A 20-week training programme was required.

Multiskilling is about developing the capacities of people to undertake a wider range of tasks and to exercise greater responsibility. It is therefore consistent with human resource management philosophy which emphasizes the importance of investing in people and, therefore, of human resource development. Multiskilling, however, makes considerable demands on the organization to provide the training required and to motivate people to learn.

Multiskilling is based on two principles as defined by Michael Cross[2]. The first is competency within the workplace, ie the ability of a single individual to assess and rectify problems as they occur day by day, regardless of the nature of the problem. The second is the full utilization of capabilities, ie the only limitations on who does what, how and when, are the skills that an individual has or can acquire, the time available to perform any new or additional tasks, and the requirements of safety.

It is necessary to set clear objectives for the levels of benefit expected from multiskilling, including better use of resources, focusing attention on critical success factors and increased productivity. It is also essential to decide how the success of multiskilling can be measured and to introduce methods of monitoring progress.

At Shell's Stanlow plant in the UK a productivity/flexibility deal was negotiated with the union in 1985 which provided for multiskilling. The progress made in implementing the deal was monitored under the following headings.

- **Attitudes to the deal**   How positive?
- **Operating**   How efficient?
- **Service to operations**   How effective?
- **Training**   How effective?
- **Representation**   Are the new representative systems working well?
- **Consultation**   Are the existing and new consultation structures working well?
- **Contractors**   How were they being used? Are their numbers reducing?
- **Overtime**   How well is it being controlled?
- **Costs**   Are targets for cost reduction being achieved?

Organization-based flexibility

Organization-based approaches to flexibility include making more use of part-time and temporary staff or contract workers. Although the evidence does not indicate that this route is being followed to any great extent, there is still scope in some situations, especially the service industries, to develop a strategy for relying on a smaller nucleus of permanent employees, the so-called core.

Pay-based flexibility

Reward policies should allow for flexibility in operating the reward system in response to business fluctuations, the rapidly changing pressures to which the organization and its employees are likely to be subjected, the demand for different types of skills and variations in market rates for different categories of staff.

Flexibility can be achieved by:

- increasing the proportion of variable performance-related pay in the total package;
- avoiding the use of rigid, hierarchical pay structures by such means as the use of pay curves, where progression is dependent on competence and performance;
- introducing skill-based pay systems to reward employees who acquire extra skills;
- not having a mechanistic system of relating rewards to performance;
- relating pay awards entirely to merit and increases in market rates, thus avoiding a separate and explicit link with increases in the cost of living, and giving scope to reward good performers more and poor performers less;
- allowing employees greater choice in the benefits they receive;
- recognizing that the organization must respond quickly to the problems caused by skill shortages and market rate pressures, and flexing the pay arrangements accordingly.

References

1. Atkinson, J (1984) 'Manpower strategies for flexible organizations', *Personnel Management*, August.
2. Cross, M (1991) 'Monitoring multiskilling: the way to guarantee long-term change', *Personnel Management*, March.

FLEXIBILITY CHECKLIST

What is the scope for improving flexibility in any of the following areas?

1. Contract-based – new forms of employment contracts.
2. Time-based – shift working and flexible hours.
3. Job-based – job-related flexibilities providing for people to carry out a wider range of activities.
4. Skills-based – multiskilling.
5. Organization-based – the use of contract workers and part-timers.
6. Pay-based – more flexible reward systems.

14

Managing conflict

Conflict is inevitable in organizations because the objectives, values and needs of groups and individuals do not always coincide. Conflict may be a sign of a healthy organization. Bland agreement on everything would be unnatural and enervating. There should be clashes of ideas about tasks and projects, and disagreements should not be suppressed. They should come out into the open because that is the only way to ensure that the issues are explored and conflicts are resolved.

There is such a thing as creative conflict. But conflict becomes counter-productive when it is based on personality clashes, or when it is treated as an unseemly mess to be hurriedly cleared away, rather than as a problem to be worked through.

Conflict resolution can be concerned with conflict between groups and conflict between individuals.

HANDLING INTER-GROUP CONFLICT

There are three principal ways of resolving inter-group conflict: peaceful coexistence, compromise and problem solving.

Peaceful coexistence

The aim here is to smooth out differences and emphasize the common ground. People are encouraged to learn to live together; there is a good deal of information, contact and exchange of views, and individuals move freely between groups (eg between headquarters and the field, or between sales and manufacturing).

This is a pleasant ideal, but it may not be practicable in many situations. There is much evidence that conflict is not necessarily resolved by getting people together. Improved communications and techniques such as briefing groups may appear to be good ideas but are useless if management has nothing to say that people want to hear. There is also the danger that the real issues, submerged for the moment in an atmosphere of superficial *bonhomie,* will surface again at a later date.

Compromise

The issue is resolved by negotiation or bargaining and neither party wins or loses. This concept of splitting the difference is essentially pessimistic. The hallmark of this approach is that there is no 'right' or 'best' answer. Agreements only accommodate differences. Real issues are not likely to be solved.

Problem solving

An attempt is made to find a genuine solution to the problem rather than just accommodating different points of view. This is where the apparent paradox of 'creative conflict' comes in. Conflict situations can be used to advantage to create better solutions.

If solutions are to be developed by problem solving, they have to be generated by those who share the responsibility for seeing that the solutions work. The sequence of actions is as follows: first, those concerned work to define the problem and agree on the objectives to be attained in reaching a solution; second, the group develops alternative solutions and debates their merits; third, agreement is reached on the preferred course of action and how it should be implemented.

HANDLING CONFLICT BETWEEN INDIVIDUALS

Handling interpersonal conflict can be even more difficult than resolving conflicts between groups. Whether the conflict is openly hostile or subtly covert, strong personal feelings may be involved. Yet, as James Ware and Louis Barnes[1] say:

> The ability to productively manage such conflict is critical to managerial success. Interpersonal differences often become sharpest when the organizational stakes seem to be high, but almost all organizations

include their share of small issues blown into major conflicts. The manager's problem is to build on human differences of opinion while not letting them jeopardize overall performance, satisfaction and growth.

Ware and Barnes go on to say that interpersonal conflict, like intergroup conflict, is an organizational reality which is neither good nor bad. It can be destructive, but it can also play a productive role. 'Problems usually arise when potential conflict is artificially suppressed, or when it escalates beyond the control of the adversaries or third-party intermediaries.'

The reaction to interpersonal conflict may be the withdrawal of either party, leaving the other one to hold the field. This is the classic win/lose situation. The problem has been resolved by force, but this may not be the best solution if it represents one person's point of view which has ignored counter-arguments, in fact, has steam-rollered over them. The winner may be triumphant but the loser will be aggrieved and either demotivated or resolved to fight again another day. There will have been a lull in, but not an end to, the conflict.

Another approach is to smooth over differences and pretend that the conflict does not exist, although no attempt has been made to tackle the root causes. Again, this is an unsatisfactory approach. The issue is likely to re-emerge and the battle will recommence.

Yet another approach is bargaining to reach a compromise. This means that both sides are prepared to lose as well as win some points and the aim is to reach a solution acceptable to both sides. Bargaining, however, involves all sorts of tactical and often counter-productive games, and the parties are often more anxious to seek acceptable compromises than to achieve sound solutions.

Ware and Barnes identify two other approaches to managing interpersonal conflict. These are controlling and constructive confrontation.

Controlling

Controlling can involve preventing interaction, or structuring the forms of interaction, or reducing or changing external pressures.

Preventing interaction is a strategy for use when emotions are high. Conflict is controlled by keeping the parties apart in the hope that, although the differences still exist, the people involved have time to cool down and consider more constructive approaches. But this may only be a temporary expedient and the eventual confrontation could be even more explosive.

Structuring the forms of interaction can be a strategy when it is not possible to separate the parties. In these cases ground rules can be developed to deal with the conflict concerning such behaviours as communicating information or dealing with specific issues. However, this may also be a temporary strategy if the strong underlying feelings are only suppressed rather than resolved.

Personal counselling is an approach which does not address the conflict itself but focuses on how the two people are reacting. Personal counselling gives people a chance to release pent-up tensions and may encourage people to think about new ways of resolving the conflict. But it does not address the essential nature of the conflict, which is the relationship between two people. That is why constructive confrontation offers the best hope of a long-term solution.

Constructive confrontation

Constructive confrontation is a method of bringing the individuals in conflict together, ideally with a third party whose function is to help build an exploratory and cooperative climate.

Constructive confrontation aims to get the parties involved to understand and explore the other party's perceptions and feelings. It is a process of developing mutual understanding to produce a win/win situation. The issues will be confronted, but on the basis of a joint analysis with the help of the third party of facts relating to the situation and the actual behaviour of those involved. Feelings will be expressed but they will be analysed by reference to specific events and behaviours rather than inferences or speculations about motives.

Third parties have a key role in this process, and it is not an easy one. They have to get agreement to the ground rules for discussions aimed at bringing out the facts and minimizing hostile behaviour. They must monitor the ways in which negative feelings are expressed, and encourage the parties to produce new definitions of the problem and its cause or causes, and new motives to reach a common solution. Third parties must avoid the temptation to support or appear to support either of those in contention. They should adopt a counselling approach, as follows:

■ listen actively;

- observe as well as listen;
- help people to understand and define the problem by asking pertinent, open-ended questions;
- recognize feelings and allow them to be expressed;
- help people to define problems for themselves;
- encourage people to explore alternative solutions;
- get people to develop their own implementation plans but provide advice and help if asked.

CONCLUSIONS

Conflict, as has been said, is in itself not to be deplored: it is an inevitable concomitant of progress and change. What is regrettable is the failure to use conflict constructively. Effective problem solving and constructive confrontation both resolve conflicts, and open up channels of discussion and cooperative action.

Many years ago one of the pioneering writers on management, Mary Parker Follett[2], wrote something on managing conflict which is as valid today as it was then:

> Differences can be made to contribute to the common cause if they are resolved by integration rather than domination or compromise.

References

1. Ware, J and Barnes, L (1991) 'Managing interpersonal conflict', in J Gabarro (ed), *Managing People and Organizations*, Harvard Business School Publications, Boston, Mass.
2. Follett, M P (1924) *Creative Experience*, Longmans Green, New York.

CONFLICT MANAGEMENT CHECKLIST

1. What is the essential nature of the conflict – what substantive issues are involved?
2. What are the apparent causes of the conflict – immediate or longer term?
3. What are the underlying or background conditions leading to the conflict or increasing its severity?

4. What are the potential immediate and longer term consequences of the conflict for the individuals or groups involved, and for the organization?
5. What behaviour patterns characterize the conflict?
6. What approach is most likely to provide for the long-term and productive resolution of the conflict:

   — problem solving to produce creative and win/win solutions; or
   — structuring the forms of interaction; or
   — reducing or changing external pressures; or
   — personal counselling; or
   — constructive confrontation which incorporates a problem-solving approach?

7. Should a third party be involved in resolving the conflict through some form of constructive confrontation and, if so, whom?
8. How should the third party approach their mediating role with particular reference to:

   — getting the real issues out into the open;
   — analysing fundamental causes;
   — dealing with facts and actual behaviours;
   — exploring feelings;
   — minimizing hostile, aggressive and generally counter-productive behaviour;
   — adopting a counselling approach, ie listening actively, observing, questioning, recognizing feelings, helping people to define the problem, exploring joint solutions, helping to implement as required?

15

Resourcing

WHAT RESOURCING IS ABOUT

Resourcing is about matching human resources to the strategic and operational needs of the organization. It is concerned with establishing what resources are required, and then satisfying those requirements through recruitment and training activities.

RESOURCING STRATEGIES

Resourcing strategies exist to provide the people and skills required to support the business strategy. They provide the basis for recruitment and training programmes. The philosophy behind them is that it is people who implement the strategic plan. The process is one of planning with people in mind.

Resourcing strategies address two fundamental questions.

1. What kind of people do we need to compete effectively, now and in the foreseeable future?
2. What do we have to do to attract, develop and keep these people?

Integrating business and resourcing strategies

The integration of business and resourcing strategies is based on an understanding of the direction in which the organization is going, and of the resulting human resource needs in terms of:

■ numbers required in relation to projected activity levels;
■ skills required on the basis of technological and product/market developments and strategies to enhance quality or reduce costs;

■ the impact of organizational restructuring;

■ plans for changing the culture of the organization which indicate the need for people with different attitudes, beliefs and personal characteristics.

RECRUITMENT PLANS

Recruitment plans are developed and implemented to meet present and forecast human resource requirements. They may have to deal specifically with skill shortages and reductions in the number of young people entering the labour market. The following approaches can be considered:

■ improving methods of identifying the sort of people the organization wants;

■ establishing better links with schools and colleges to gain their interest;

■ liaising closely with local training organizations – in the UK this will mean the local TEC (Training Enterprise Council);

■ developing career programmes and training packages to attract young people;

■ widening the recruitment net to include, for example, more women entering the labour market;

■ finding ways of tapping alternative pools of suitable employees;

■ adapting working hours and arrangements to the needs of new employees;

■ providing more attractive benefit packages;

■ providing child-care facilities;

■ developing the talents and making better use of existing employees;

■ providing retraining to develop different skills;

■ making more effort to retain staff.

TRAINING

Training strategies should be designed to improve organizational effectiveness by developing individual competences and enlarging the skill base. They should lead to the use of planned training approaches and an emphasis on performance-related training.

Planned training

Planned training is a deliberate intervention aimed at achieving the learning necessary for improved job performance. The process of planned training consists of the following steps.

1. **Identify and define training needs** This involves analysing corporate, team, occupational and individual needs to acquire new skills or knowledge, or to improve existing competences (competence is defined as the ability and willingness to perform a task). The analysis covers problems to be solved as well as future demands. Decisions are made at this stage on the extent to which training is the best and most cost-effective way to solve the problem.
2. **Define the learning required** It is necessary to specify as clearly as possible what skills and knowledge have to be learnt, and what attitudes need to be developed.
3. **Define the objectives of training** Learning objectives are set which define not only what has to be learnt but also what trainees must be able to do after their training programme.
4. **Plan training programmes** These must be developed to meet the needs and objectives by using the right combination of training techniques and locations.
5. **Decide who provides the training** The extent to which training is provided from within or outside the organization will be decided. At the same time, the decision of responsibility between the training department, managers or supervisors and individuals has to be determined.
6. **Implement the training** Ensure that the most appropriate methods are used.

Performance-related training

A performance-related approach to training relates training specifically to performance requirements. For individuals this may mean filling gaps between what they know and *can* do, and what they should know and be able to do. But concentrating on filling gaps may mean falling into the trap of adopting the 'deficiency model' of training which implies that training is only about putting right the things that have gone wrong.

Training is much more positive than that. It is, or should be, primarily concerned with identifying and satisfying development needs – multiskilling, fitting people to take on extra responsibility, providing for management succession and increasing all-round competence.

Performance-related training also relates to organizational needs. These will be concerned with ensuring that employees have the necessary knowledge and skills to be able to take on new tasks as the company grows, diversifies, develops new products, markets and operational systems, and introduces new technology.

Performance-related training is competence based. It starts from an analysis of the competences required for successful performance – now and in the future, assesses the areas in which competences need to be developed, and plans and installs training programmes or processes such as performance management to create the levels of competence required.

RESOURCING CHECKLIST

Resourcing strategy

1. Have human resource requirements been established to match strategic plans?

Recruitment

2. Have specifications been prepared spelling out requirements in terms of the skills and competences needed for effective job performance?
3. Have the strengths and weaknesses of the organization as an employer been analysed in such areas as pay, opportunity, security, intrinsic interest of the work, training and career prospects? And have steps been taken to make the best of the strengths and overcome the weaknesses?
4. Is the best use made of all possible sources of human resource requirements covering internal training and promotion as well as a range of external sources?
5. Are interviewers properly trained and briefed?
6. Is use made of suitable selection tests?

7. Are follow-up studies conducted to validate the selection procedure?
8. In general, is the organization able to attract and retain the quantity and quality of people it needs?

Training

9. Has the organization clearly defined policies covering the objectives of training, the scope of training schemes, the amount to be spent on training, and guidance on the responsibility for training of line managers and team leaders?
10. Do training plans and programmes cater for the training needs of all categories of employees, and for the need to expand the skill base of the organization?
11. Do the plans and programmes cater specifically for the skills required following the introduction of new technology and for the needs for multiskilling and flexibility?
12. Is proper attention paid to the importance of learning on the job, as well as by means of formal training courses?
13. Is encouragement and help given to employees to obtain National Vocational Qualifications (NVQs) based on standards of occupational competence founded on best practice in the workplace?
14. Are the principles of the Management Charter Initiative applied to management training, ie the use of crediting competence processes based on the principle that people continue to learn on a practical level throughout their working lives, long after completing their formal education and training?
15. Are 'contract learning' processes used which involve written agreements between learners, their managers and tutors on the achievement of specified learning objectives?
16. Are 'mentors' provided to complement formal training programmes by providing individuals with additional guidance and advice?
17. Is an 'action learning' approach used to help managers learn by being exposed to real problems?

18. Are managers and team leaders fully aware of their training responsibilities, and do they carry them out effectively?
19. Is it generally appreciated that, although formal 'off-the-job' training courses have their part to play, the best form of development is self-development, given proper support and encouragement by the organization and the immediate manager?
20. Are training needs identified systematically by training surveys, analyses of new skill requirements, skills analysis processes and performance management reviews?
21. Is the effectiveness of training evaluated systematically?

16

Continuous improvement – creating a learning organization

The concept of continuous improvement is based on the assumption that striving continually to reach higher and higher standards in every part of the organization will provide a series of incremental gains that will build superior performance. In Japan the process is called *kaizen*, and consists of the organization creating an environment in which all employees can contribute to improving performance and overall effectiveness as a normal and continuing part of their job.

In an environment dedicated to continuous improvement such as that developed at Nissan[1], managers and team leaders have as a prime objective the bringing out of new ideas and concepts from their staff. Their task is to create an environment in which new thinking is encouraged and welcomed. The management of Nissan believes that it is part of everyone's job to improve continually. This is embedded in the organization as a fundamental value, not by exhortation but by practical steps such as workshops, where employees with ideas for new tooling or other changes can go to try them out. The supervisor is expected to lead problem solving and continuous improvement activities, but as experience develops, other team members will assume responsibility for improvement groups. It is accepted by managers and supervisors that they have no monopoly of wisdom on the best uses of performing a task or making improvements. This is on the basis that the person actually doing the work is likely to know much more about the problem than they do.

By methods such as these, and by constant emphasis at all levels on its importance, continuous improvement can become a way of life in an organization. It can, and should, be one of its key values, which is reflected in the way everyone behaves, and is underpinned by such processes as performance and reward management, where ability to stimulate and achieve improvements will be an important criterion for assessing and rewarding performance.

The development of a culture of continuous improvement, however, is also fostered if the enterprise functions as a learning organization and implements continuous development policies.

THE LEARNING ORGANIZATION

A learning organization has been defined by Pedler et al[2] as 'an organization which facilitates the learning of all its members and continually transforms itself'.

Bob Garratt[3] has pointed out that the decline in the ranks of middle managers as companies adopt a flatter and more customer-responsive profile requires senior managers to adopt a much clearer strategic role, which places a premium on flexibility, responsiveness and learning. Such managers have to develop their own learning abilities, and work and learn as teams. It is also necessary to develop a climate and processes which enable an organization to learn; these include job enlargement and enrichment, mentoring, and various forms of team and project-based work.

Ed Schein[4] looks at learning organizations in terms of managers. He sees their careers developing over a period of time in a series of deals with employing organizations and outlines three stages to this process. First, the organization produced strategic plans which define future managerial work. This includes an analysis of the organization structure within which the work will be completed, together with a definition of the roles that will need to be filled. Second, managers think through key issues which affect them as individuals. These include an assessment of what they want from life, the role of work within that and the formulation of feasible personal career plans. Third, there is an information exchange in which the organization outlines requirements and opportunities for the future, and individual managers explain personal needs and career aims.

John Burgoyne[5] states that a learning organization channels the career and life-planning energies of individual managers in a way that allows the organization to meet its strategic needs. This is done through a combination of factors: encouraging the identification of individual needs; the organic formulation of business strategy with inputs from training departments in current skills; and continued organizational review and learning from experience. He suggests that to operate effectively as a learning organization, its managers should have a complete understanding of its problems, an ability to respond with flexibility to changing situations, a moral and ethical approach to management, and the ability to learn and apply learning.

According to Alan Mumford[6], the characteristics of a learning organization are that it:

- encourages managers and staff to identify their own learning needs;
- provides a regular review of performance and learning for the individual;
- encourages employees to set challenging learning goals for themselves;
- provides feedback at the time on both performance and achieved learning;
- reviews the performance of managers in helping to develop others;
- assists employees to see learning opportunities on the job;
- seeks to provide new experiences from which people can learn;
- provides or facilitates on-the-job training;
- tolerates some mistakes, provided people try to learn from them;
- encourages managers to review, conclude and plan learning activities;
- encourages people to challenge the traditional ways of doing things.

Charles Handy[7] points out that a learning organization can and should mean two things; it can mean an organization which learns and/or an organization which encourages learning in its people. He believes that a learning organization needs a formal way of asking questions, seeking out theories, testing them and reflecting upon them. The learning organization constantly reframes the world and its part in it. Members of the organization are encouraged to suggest improvements. The organization has to find answers to questions about its strengths and talents, its weaknesses and what sort of organization it wants to be. It also has to cultivate its 'negative capability', ie its capacity to learn from its mistakes.

Explicit steps are taken by learning organizations to learn from experience. They provide various forums such as development centres, team meetings, 'away day' conferences and workshops to enable people to reflect on what they have learned and what they still need to learn. Such reflections provide a basis for formulating organizational and individual improvement plans.

A learning organization will be concerned with the development of skills and competences at all levels, emphasizing the importance of learning by informal means on the job with the help and guidance of managers and colleagues. The importance will be recognized of what Alan Mumford calls 'incidental learning' – the learning that can be built around incidents in everyone's day-to-day working life and career. Performance management, as described in Chapter 17, is a process which can systematize this incidental learning by providing for the review of achievements in relation to agreed objectives and the analysis of the behaviours which have contributed to success or failure.

A more structured, educational approach can be adopted, as at British Telecom where David Beard[8] reported that the model through which its UK sales force has become a 'learning organization' involves three levels of learning, applying and developing. The first level is individual; participants attend a development centre, review their performance and abilities, and apply the learning to their work and career development. This is completed on a regular basis and includes reviews with line managers. The second level deals with teams; team managers facilitate team reviews through team meetings and coaching. The third level is organizational and involves learning, reviewing and developing by the top management team, with inputs from the other two levels.

These sorts of approaches are closely linked to the concept of continuous development, as described below.

CONTINUOUS DEVELOPMENT

A philosophy of continuing development states that training is not just something that is provided for people by the organization at the start of their employment or at occasional points in their career. It should instead be regarded as a continuous process, with less emphasis on formal instruction and an increased requirement for trainees to be responsible for their own learning. This has led to the development of such approaches as 'do-it-yourself training', action learning and computer-based training.

The Institute of Personnel Management's 1987 code of practice on continuous development states:

> If learning activity in an organization is to be fully beneficial both to the organization and its employees, the following conditions must be met:
>
> ■ the organization must have some form of strategic business plan – it is desirable that the implications of the strategic plan, in terms of the skills and knowledge of the employees who will achieve it, should be spelled out;
> ■ managers must be ready and willing (and able) to define and meet needs as they appear; all learning needs cannot be anticipated – organizations must foster a philosophy of continuous development;
> ■ as far as practicable, learning and work must be integrated – this means that encouragement must be given to all employees to learn from the problems, challenges and successes inherent in their day-to-day actvities;
> ■ the impetus for continuous development must come from the chief executive and other members of the top management team (the board of directors, for example) – the top management team must regularly and formally review the way the competence of its management and workforce is being developed;
> ■ one senior executive should have the responsibility for ensuring that continuous development activity is being effectively undertaken;
> ■ investment in continuous development must be regarded by the top management team as being as important as investment in research, new product development or capital equipment – it is not a luxury which can be afforded only in the 'good times'. Indeed, the more severe the problems an organization faces the greater the need for learning on the part of its employees and the more pressing the need for investment in learning.

Money spent within the organization on research and development into human resource development itself is money well spent. An evaluation of current human resource development procedures can confirm the effectiveness of current practice or point the way towards necessary change. Such research is as valuable as technical research.

References

1. Wickens, P (1987) *The Road to Nissan*, Macmillan, London.
2. Pedler, M, Boydell, T and Burgoyne, J (1989) 'Towards the learning company', *Management Education and Development*, vol **20**: 1.

3. Garratt, R (1990) *Creating a Learning Organization*, Institute of Directors, London.

4. Schein, E (1977) *Career Dynamics*, Addison-Wesley, Reading, Mass.

5. Burgoyne, J (1988) 'Management development for the individual *and* the organization', *Personnel Management*, June.

6. Mumford, A (1989) *Management Development: Strategies for Action, Institute of Personnel Management*, London.

7. Handy, C (1989) *The Age of Unreason*, Business Books, London.

8. Beard, D (1993) 'Learning to change organizations', *Personnel Management*, January.

CONTINUOUS IMPROVEMENT CHECKLIST

1. Does the culture of the organization support and encourage new thinking, and the involvement of employees at all levels in problem solving and seeking improvements?

2. Is the capacity to involve people in seeking improvements, and getting new ideas accepted, recognized and rewarded appropriately?

3. Are people encouraged to challenge traditional ways of doing things?

4. Are steps taken by the organization to ensure that the top management and employees at all levels have the 'space', and are encouraged to reflect on their experiences and learn from them?

5. Are managers and individuals encouraged to identify their own learning needs and to set learning goals for themselves?

6. Are managers and staff encouraged to see learning opportunities in their day-to-day work?

7. Are systematic efforts made by the organization and its managers to provide new experiences from which employees can learn?

8. Are people encouraged to learn from their mistakes as well as their successes?

9. Are forums (meetings, conferences etc) provided for people to learn from their experiences and develop improvement plans?

10. Are managers encouraged to define and meet learning needs as they appear?

17

Performance management

DEFINITION

Performance management is a means of getting better results from the organization, teams and individuals by understanding and managing performance within an agreed framework of planned goals, objectives, and standards of achievement and competence.

It can be defined as a process or set of processes for establishing shared understanding about what *is* to be achieved, and of managing and developing people in a way which increases the probability that it *will* be achieved in the short and longer term.

Perhaps the most important thing to remember about performance management is that it is a *continuous* process shared between managers and the people for whom they are responsible. It is about improving both results and the quality of working relationships. Good performance management means that people are clear about what their priorities are, what they should be doing currently, what they should be aiming for, the level of competence they should achieve, and how well this contributes to both team and company performance. It grows from open, positive and constructive discussion between managers, individuals and teams to produce agreement on how to focus on doing the job better.

BASIS

The philosophy of performance management is strongly influenced by the belief that it is a natural process of management. Its emphasis on analysis, measurement, monitoring performance and planning for performance improvements means that it is concerned with basic aspects of good practice with regard to the management of people. It is a system which should be driven by management so that it becomes part of their everyday working life and not an annual chore imposed upon them by the personnel department.

Performance management systems can help managers, in Charles Handy's[1] words, to:

- be teachers, counsellors and friends, as much or more than they are commanders, counsellors and judges;
- trust people to use their own methods to achieve the manager's own ends;
- delegate on the basis of a positive will to trust and to enable, and a willingness to be trusted and enabled;
- become 'post-heroic' leaders who know that every problem can be solved in such a way as to develop other people's capacity to handle it.

THE PROCESS OF PERFORMANCE MANAGEMENT

Performance management starts at the top level in an organization with definitions of mission, strategy and objectives. These lead to more detailed definitions of functional or departmental missions, plans and objectives.

Performance agreements

Performance agreements are then made between individuals and their managers which set out:

- the key result areas of the job;
- the objectives and standards of performance associated with these key result areas;
- work and personal development plans;
- the skills and behaviours required to fulfil job requirements.

Continuous review

The performance of individuals and their development is reviewed continuously as part of the normal process of management. It is not deferred until a formal performance review takes place at the end of the year when it will have lost its immediacy and where the relative formality of the proceedings may prevent a constructive discussion.

Effective performance is reinforced with praise, recognition and the opportunity to take on more responsible work. Less effective performance is dealt with as it happens by reiterating the standards and competences required, indicating areas for improvement and agreeing the actions required to affect improvements. Coaching and counselling is provided as necessary.

Formal performance review

There is a periodic formal review which, in effect, is a stocktaking exercise, but its emphasis is on looking forward to the next period and redefining the performance agreement rather than raking over past events. The review is concerned with three aspects of the individual's performance (the three 'Cs'):

- **contribution** what the individual has achieved in relation to the objectives, performance standards and work plans contained in the performance agreement, and the contribution the individual has made to achieving team, departmental and organizational objectives;
- **competence** the level of competence reached by the individual in each area of the job as specified in the performance agreement;
- **continuous development** the progress the individual is making in developing skills and competences and in improving performance on a continuing basis.

The review leads to a revised performance agreement. It also provides individuals with the opportunity to raise any concerns they have about their work and future.

Reference

1. Handy, C (1989) *The Age of Unreason*, Business Books, London.

PERFORMANCE MANAGEMENT CHECKLIST

1. Is there a system for measuring performance in relation to agreed objectives which extends to all employees?
2. Does the system assess inputs in the shape of levels of competence, as well as outputs in the form of contribution?
3. Are performance agreements concluded which set out agreed objectives and competences, and performance improvement and development plans?
4. To what extent is the system primarily developmental (ie concerned with identifying training needs and providing the basis for performance improvements), as distinct from being mainly used as a basis for determining performance-related pay increases?
5. If a rating system is used, is it based on achievements in relation to clear performance criteria?
6. Do staff generally think that performance ratings are fair?
7. Is it recognized that performance management is a continuous process and not simply a once a year event?
8. Are performance review meetings conducted well by managers with particular regard to:

   — proper preparation;
   — creating the right atmosphere;
   — working to a clear structure;
   — using praise judicially;
   — letting individuals do most of the talking;
   — inviting self-appraisal;
   — discussing performance not personality;
   — encouraging analysis of performance;
   — not delivering unexpected criticisms;
   — agreeing objectives, performance management and plans of action?

9. Is performance management used as a basis for identifying training needs?
10. Are managers and staff committed to the performance management system?

18

Productivity management

Better productivity leading to lower costs in relation to output is an essential characteristic of an effective organization. But it does not happen of its own accord – it has to be planned for and worked at. Before looking at the productivity audit, the essential base for a productivity programme, it is necessary to define productivity and discuss how it is measured.

WHAT IS PRODUCTIVITY?

Productivity is the relationship between the input and output of goods or services. It can be defined as a series of ratios:

$$\text{productivity index} = \frac{\text{output obtained}}{\text{input expected}} = \frac{\text{performance achieved}}{\text{resources consumed}} = \frac{\text{effectiveness}}{\text{efficiency}}$$

High productivity reflects the full (ie effective and efficient) use of resources. Usually one thinks of human resources in connection with productivity, but other resources such as money, materials, machinery, systems and time, are all relevant and affect the rate of productivity achieved.

HOW IS PRODUCTIVITY MEASURED?

Measuring productivity is not easy. Work processes are often complex and a clearly definable unit of output against which an input of costs can be compared may not be available. Physical quantities can be expressed in financial terms (eg the sales value of production), but this is a somewhat more remote measure than that of cost per unit of output. Furthermore, measurements often concentrate on activities rather than output, and this 'activity trap' can lead to over-concentration on the activities themselves rather than on what they are there to achieve. The first step in measuring productivity is therefore to find a way of quantifying the results expected – if possible in physical terms but, if not, in terms of sales values.

Bearing in mind that productivity is not simply performance and not simply the economic use of resources, but a combination of both, the task is to find ratios which include both variables.

1. Input variables will include payroll costs, the associated costs of employment, the number of people employed and the number of hours worked or time taken.
2. Output variables will include units produced, products sold, tasks completed, revenues obtained, value added, responsibilities met and standards reached (including standard hours produced).

A wide variety of productivity ratios can be derived from these input and output variables, and these can be analysed and added to under headings such as the examples given below.

1. **Output ratios**

    — $\dfrac{\text{units produced or processed}}{\text{number of employees}}$

    — $\dfrac{\text{sales turnover}}{\text{number of employees}}$

2. **Cost ratios**

    — $\dfrac{\text{wages cost}}{\text{units produced}}$

    — $\dfrac{\text{sales turnover}}{\text{payroll/employment costs}}$

Having established how productivity should be measured, the next step is to conduct a productivity audit and then prepare a productivity improvement programme.

THE PRODUCTIVITY AUDIT

The aim of the productivity audit should be to establish what the facts are, why any problems have arisen and how those problems should be solved. The main steps to be taken in conducting a productivity audit are:

1. define terms of reference;
2. select the individual responsible for the audit;
3. ensure that resources are available to conduct the audit;
4. select the ratios to be used for measuring productivity;
5. define the standards to be achieved;
6. identify the information required and how and from where it is to be obtained;
7. obtain the information required;
8. analyse the information in terms of ratios and standards, comparing actuals with desirable ratios or standards and with previous trends;
9. wherever the actuals are not meeting the standards or there are any adverse trends, identify the problem areas;
10. analyse the problems to determine their causes, concentrate on delving hard in order to identify the root cause and do not be content with looking at symptoms only.

A checklist for use in conducting a productivity audit is set out at the end of this chapter.

THE PRODUCTIVITY IMPROVEMENT PLAN

The productivity improvement plan identifies needs for improvement and how they should be satisfied. It will be based on the productivity audit, and the areas for consideration will be employee utilization and costs, the use of new technology, improved efficiency of production or administration, cost control and the elimination of wasteful activities.

Employee utilization and costs

The overall aim will be to ensure that each person employed provides added value. This is achieved by taking steps to improve output per employee without sacrificing quality. Improvement is partly a matter of motivation through reward management, but it also depends on leadership, the provision of work systems which will enable employees to work more effectively, the design of jobs which in themselves enable employees to raise their performance levels and the development of high-performance teams (see Chapter 12).

A productivity plan will look at the number of employees in managerial, staff, support and other jobs who do not contribute directly to production, sales or service delivery. Jobs which do not add value would be eliminated, using natural wastage and voluntary redundancy wherever possible. This process of downsizing may include stripping out unnecessary layers of management. The number of headquarters staff could be reduced to the minimum required to support the strategic planning and control functions of top management, and to provide service functions for the organization (but only when it is more effective to centralize them). Unnecessary or duplicated staff or service functions could be eliminated.

New technology and systems of work

New technology is clearly a major potential source of improvements in productivity. It can take such forms as information technology to improve the flow of control information and eliminate routine work, automation, and computerized production and inventory control systems.

New systems of work can include just-in-time, to minimize stock levels and speed up production, and flexible manufacturing, which makes use of computer numerically controlled machines in cells to increase flexibility and maximize the contribution that can be made by individual employees working in high-performance teams.

Efficiency

Improved efficiency can be achieved by streamlining production, operational and administrative systems. This can be done by method study and by techniques such as variety reduction, which involves the analysis of products or components in order to minimize the variety of products, parts, materials or processing operations.

Paperwork can be reduced by relying much more on on-line personal computers, and by eliminating unnecessary reports and forms.

Cost control

Cost control is a matter of reducing employment costs (which can amount to 50 per cent or more of total company costs), improving efficiency and minimizing waste.

Value analysis can be used to identify and eliminate unnecessary cost elements in a component or product.

A cost reduction exercise should be aimed at achieving targets for reducing overheads, employment costs, processing costs, and the costs of materials and inventory.

Waste control

An attack should be made on all forms of waste in manufacturing and offices. All paperwork routines should be challenged, and unnecessary forms and reports eliminated. Particular attention should be paid to analysing manufacturing processes and the control exercised over manufacturing operations to identify and remove wasteful practices.

Implementation

The programme for improving productivity must be run by top management in that they should set the objectives, define terms of reference, appoint the executive responsible for the programme, provide them with the resources needed and monitor the results achieved.

A senior manager responsible directly to the chief executive should be in charge of the programme. Avoid committees. They spend their time talking, not doing. The productivity executive will need help – from computer, work study, personnel and finance departments – but they should get these departments involved directly rather than sitting them round a table to talk to one another. It may be helpful to set up small project teams comprising members of different departments to carry out tasks, but they should be given specific things to do and achieve, and strict deadlines.

It is important at this stage to involve employees and consult with trade unions. Much more can be achieved with their cooperation, which could take the form of improvement or productivity groups charged with implementing specified parts of the programme (the considerations to be taken into account when introducing new technology are discussed in Chapter 21). It is essential to ensure that everyone concerned knows what is being done, why it is being done, how it will affect them and how they can help to make it a success.

Having decided whom is going to be involved and how, the next steps are to decide on the methods to be used, the results expected (targets to be achieved) and the timetable. The costs and benefits of the whole exercise should also be determined.

A system should be set up for monitoring the implementation of the programme so that steps can be taken to ensure that:

- the programme is going according to plan;
- the expected results are being achieved;
- the programme is amended to meet changing conditions or to correct a deviation from the plan or a failure to meet it.

Procedures should also be created for monitoring productivity continually so that the achievements of the initial programme are consolidated and improved upon.

What are the factors for success?

A successful productivity improvement programme depends on:

1. a well-planned programme based on a productivity audit, with positive objectives and a clearly defined timetable;
2. a commitment on the part of management to the programme;
3. employees who are involved in the programme and are prepared, with suitable safeguards concerning their future, to participate in implementing it;
4. a recognition that the benefits resulting from the programme should be shared among everyone concerned – the organization, management and all other employees.

These are demanding criteria for success; they are not easily achieved and things can go wrong. Managers, supervisors and other employees will all be suspicious of the programme. They will see it either as a device for exposing their inadequacies, an instrument for unacceptable change or a threat to their livelihood. Of course, productivity improvement plans can result in downsizing, but it is essential to take whatever steps are possible to mitigate unpleasant consequences through such means as redeployment, retraining and reducing numbers by natural wastage or voluntary redundancy.

Communication, education, involvement and persuasion are essential aspects of the programme.

Even if persuasion and the involvement of employees in the programme are sufficient to overcome their natural resistance to change, there are still a number of problems to be avoided in implementing productivity improvements. These include:

1. making recommendations based on inaccurate information or conclusions;
2. making recommendations on new equipment, methods or procedures without properly evaluating the cost-effectiveness of the proposals;
3. making recommendations without properly evaluating the impact of changes on other departments;
4. proposing changes without giving sufficient consideration to the reactions of those involved.

These mistakes are frequently made and they are all avoidable. Those responsible for productivity improvement programmes will be much less likely to commit these errors if they are made aware of the dangers in advance.

PRODUCTIVITY CHECKLIST

Performance

1. What are the levels of productivity being achieved compared with targets?
2. How do these levels compare with other benchmark organizations?

Control

3. Are control reports clearly identifying variances and deviations from the plan?
4. Are individuals fully accountable for failures to achieve targets or standards?
5. Is prompt corrective action taken by management to correct adverse variances or results?

Work methods

6. Is a there an effective policy of continuous improvement covering all aspects of the work of the organization?

Work measurement

7. Is work measurement used wherever feasible to develop standards, give better control information, and improve methods and procedures?
8. Is work measurement used to provide the basis for effective incentive schemes?

New technology

9. Is there a constant search by management for ways of improving productivity by the use of new technology, including computerization and automation?
10. Is investment in equipment or machinery justified on a cost benefit basis?
11. Is the use of existing equipment managed to achieve maximum productivity?

Management

12. Is management fully conscious of the need for productivity?
13. Are management and supervisors taking active and successful steps to improve the productivity consciousness of their staff?
14. Is productivity performance treated as a key criterion in assessing the capabilities and rewards of management and supervisors?
15. Does the organization of work ensure that decision taking on key aspects of productivity is taken at the point where work is carried out and the impact is greatest?
16. Is research into methods of improving productivity an important function in the organization?

Motivation and involvement

17. Are employees motivated effectively by management and supervisors to achieve greater productivity?
18. Is a continuous review carried out by management on ways of improving motivation for productivity?
19. Are employees involved in seeking ways of improving productivity?
20. Do employees appreciate that improvements in productivity benefit themselves as well as the company?

Pay

21. Are payment by results schemes used wherever possible to boost productivity?
22. Are payment by results schemes kept under close review to ensure that they are cost-effective?
23. Are rewards to those not on payment by results schemes related to achievement and contribution?
24. Are schemes for sharing the rewards from increased productivity among employees used to promote further gains in productivity?

Restrictive practices

25. Have agreements been negotiated with trade unions to buy out restrictive practices?
26. Are the agreements cost-effective in that the value of improvements in productivity resulting from the elimination of restrictive practices outweighs the cost of buying them out?

Training

27. Have analyses of training needs concentrated on ways of improving productivity, for example by improving flexibility and multiskilling?
28. Have training programmes been derived from the analysis of productivity training needs?
29. Are all those who can benefit from training to improve their productivity, especially new employees, given such training?

30. Is the impact of training followed up to ensure that it is cost-effective, ie gains in productivity resulting from training outweigh the cost of that training?

Elimination of waste

31. Is there a continuous attack led by top management on all forms of excessive manpower costs and wasteful use of manpower?
32. Is work and method study used to improve the use of people by introducing more efficient techniques, systems and procedures?

Employment levels

33. Is the enlargement of staff and support departments and the engagement of indirect workers, rigidly controlled?
34. Are managers and supervisors held strictly accountable for wasteful practices?
35. Have steps been taken to strip out unnecessary layers of management, to reduce the size of support or staff departments in head office and elsewhere, and to minimize the number of indirect workers?

19

Managing quality

Competitive edge is built in many ways: by innovation, by aggressive marketing, by effective cost control, by efficiency in manufacturing, distribution or the provision of a service, by a systematic approach to performance management, and by developing a competent, well-motivated and committed workforce. Transcending all these, however, is the need for everyone in the organization to pursue excellence and this means generating a commitment to quality through processes of total quality management.

DEFINITION OF TOTAL QUALITY MANAGEMENT

Total quality management (TQM) is a systematic way of guaranteeing that all activities within an organization happen the way they have been planned in order to meet the defined needs of customers and clients. The emphasis is on involving everyone in the organization in activities which provide for continuous improvement and for achieving sustained high levels of quality performance.

THE TQM APPROACH

The TQM approach is about gaining commitment to quality. Everyone at every level in the organization has genuinely to believe in quality and to act on that belief. Total quality can be described as an attitude of mind which leads to appropriate behaviour and actions. It has to be, as at Nissan: 'the centrepiece of the company's philosophy, with commitment at every level to a zero-defect product'.[1]

Total quality should be distinguished from the quality assurance standard (BS 5750 or ISO 9000). As a quality assurance standard BS 5750 lays down the requirements for a quality management system and provides a structured approach upon which to base that system. It gives a framework for establishing quality standards and can operate as a kite mark to demonstrate that quality assurance is being tracked systematically by management. But it does not specify quality standards for products and in itself it does not guarantee the commitment of everybody in an organization to a quality programme.

BASIC CONCEPTS OF TQM

Total quality management is essentially about customer satisfaction, the importance of a 'total' approach to quality and the significance of the internal customer.

Customer satisfaction

The only real measure of the quality of a product or service is the extent to which it delivers customer satisfaction. The word 'satisfaction' can be defined as the time when all customers' wants, needs and expectations are met, whether or not they have been expressed.

The significance of internal customers

Another key concept in total quality is the significance of the internal customer. This refers to the fact that everyone who receives goods or services from a colleague within an organization is a customer of that colleague. The goods or services can include materials, tools, parts, sub assemblies, completed goods for dispatch, designs, drawings, information, advice, help, guidance, administrative assistance and so on. Suppliers of these goods and services have to be just as aware of the need to achieve high levels of quality for their colleagues as for their ultimate customers. In the last analysis, of course, the quality of the services provided to internal customers will affect the quality delivered to the external customer. But the final result can only be guaranteed if attention is paid to quality in all aspects of the transactions and processes which take place within the organization.

Total quality

The concept of total quality indicates the requirement for all employees in the organization to be involved all the time in meeting all customer requirements.

THE DEVELOPMENT OF TQM

TQM must, by definition, extend to all aspects of a company's operation, and its relationships with internal and external customers. It is essentially a process, a way of doing things, which makes use of a number of techniques but ultimately depends on the attitudes and behaviour of all those involved; and that means everyone in the organization and its suppliers.

The steps required to develop TQM are described below.

1. *Formulate a TQM policy*
    A TQM policy might cover the following points:

    ■ the goal of the organization is to achieve customer satisfaction by meeting the requirements of both external and internal customers;
    ■ the need is to establish customer requirements and respond quickly and effectively to them;
    ■ it is essential to concentrate on prevention rather than cure;
    ■ everyone is involved – all work done by company employees, suppliers and product outlets is part of a process which creates a product or service for a customer;
    ■ each employee is a customer for work done by other employees, and has the right to expect good work from them and the obligation to contribute work of high calibre to them;
    ■ the standard of quality is 'zero defect' or 'no failures' – everyone has to understand the standards required and the need to do it right first time;
    ■ sustained quality excellence requires continuous improvement;
    ■ quality performance and costs should be measured systematically;
    ■ continuous attention must be paid to satisfying educational and training needs;
    ■ high quality performance will be recognized and rewarded;
    ■ quality improvement is best achieved by the joint efforts of management and employees.
2. *Determine quality standards*
    Quality standards may simply be expressed as a zero defect policy but it is still necessary to define what a zero defect situation is for each key operation and service. This means the clarification of what constitutes a defect or failure to achieve a standard, how that will be measured or recognized and what steps may be required to prevent the occurrence of the defect.

3. *Measure quality*

   The measurement of quality may involve process control or similar techniques which include the analysis of the system, the collection of information on variations from the norm or attributes (data on whether a process is meeting or not meeting specification) and the use of techniques for establishing process capability and performance.

4. *Determine the cost of quality*

   The process of identifying the cost of total quality is a key element in understanding where existing processes are failing so that the attention of management can be focused on the achievement of noticeable improvements. The costs of quality were identified by Ron Collard[2] under five headings:

   ■ **cost of prevention** the cost of an action to prevent or reduce defects and failures;
   ■ **cost of appraisal** the cost of assessing the quality achieved;
   ■ **cost of internal failure** the costs arising within the organization due to failure to achieve the quality specified before the transfer of ownership to the customer;
   ■ **cost of external failure** the costs arising outside the organization due to failure to achieve the quality specified after the transfer of ownership to the customer;
   ■ **cost of lost opportunity** the cost of losing the opportunity to sell to customers in the future if customers have been lost through poor quality products or services.

5. *Plan for quality*

   Planning for quality involves:

   ■ recording the series of events and activities constituting the total process by the use of flow charting and other means of activity analysis;
   ■ analysing the existing processes and system flows to establish inconsistencies and potential sources of variations and defects;
   ■ specifying for each activity the necessary quality-related activities, including material and packaging specifications, quality control procedures, process control systems, and sampling and inspection procedures;
   ■ developing, as appropriate, just-in-time (JIT) systems which provide for the right quantities to be produced or delivered at the right time and ensure that there is no waste;

- determining how to achieve quality in the purchasing system, with particular reference to the development of long-term relationships with suppliers so that dependable product quality and delivery standards can be defined and maintained;
- conducting failure mode, effect and criticality studies (FMECA) to determine possible modes of failure and their effects on the performance of the produce or service, and to establish which features of product design, production or operation are critical to the various modes of failure;
- developing planned maintenance systems to reduce the incidence of emergency maintenance;
- designing quality into the product, making sure that the standards and specifications meet customer needs and can be achieved by existing processes (or, if not, by improving these processes in particular ways);
- conducting process capability studies to ensure that it will be possible to achieve quality standards through existing processes or, if not, what changes are required;
- examining quality requirements in manufacturing to ensure that answers can be made to the following questions:

  — can we make it OK?
  — are we making it OK?
  — have we made it OK?
  — could we make it better?

- studying storage, distribution and delivery arrangements to ensure that they are capable of meeting customer demands
- examining after-sales service procedures and achievements to identify areas for improvement.

Organize for quality

Organizing for quality means looking at the accountabilities of each member of the organization and ensuring that the responsibility for quality performance is clearly specified.

The organization for quality should aim to take account of the development of joint responsibility for quality in work teams. The focus should be on teamwork for quality.

Finally, consideration should be made to giving responsibility to individuals and/or task forces to oversee the development and implementation of total quality management.

Train for quality

The achievement of improved standards of quality will require additional and higher levels of skills and knowledge. Training needs therefore have to be identified and continuous training programmes developed – quality training is not a one-off process. The employee development system has to operate within a learning, self-development, continuous improvement culture.

Gain commitment to quality

Procedures and systems for laying down standards and measuring quality performance are all very well, but significant results from TQM will not be obtained unless total commitment to quality is achieved at all levels of the organization. The emphasis should be on self-responsibility for quality. This can be a long-term process – it will not be achieved by running a few short courses. Commitment is achieved by example from the top and, more importantly, by getting people involved in quality improvement programmes. Quality circles or improvement groups are one approach to achieving commitment. But they will not succeed by themselves. Total quality has to be seen as a permanent and fundamental part of everyday working. The Japanese approach, as translated to Nissan, involves seeing quality as a team affair to be discussed by all members at five-minute meetings at the start of every day.

Motivate for quality

Motivating for quality means reviewing the reward system so that it supports the strategic objectives of the total quality programme. If the system is essentially production-driven and based on individual rewards, it is likely to conflict with a quality-driven teamwork approach. The reward system should not just include financial rewards. There are other means of rewarding people by non-financial means such as recognizing achievements and providing additional learning and promotion opportunities.

BENEFITS OF TQM

The benefits of TQM include:

- increased customer satisfaction and therefore additional sales;
- the achievement of competitive advantage – companies are increasingly competing on the basis of quality products and services;

- the minimization of waste;
- the ability to redeploy resources to add real value;
- focusing attention on continuous improvement.

Overall, the process of developing a TQM culture can increase involvement, identification and commitment.

References

1. Wickens, P (1987) *The Road to Nissan*, Macmillan, London.
2. Collard, R (1992) 'Total quality: the role of human resources', in M Armstrong (ed), *Strategies for Human Resource Management*, Kogan Page, London.

MANAGING FOR QUALITY CHECKLIST

1. Is the achievement of high levels of quality recognized as one of the most important values of the organization?
2. Are quality objectives included in strategic plans?
3. Is the achievement of quality objectives and standards regarded as a key criterion for assessing performance?
4. Is there total commitment and support from the top to total quality?
5. Is there a policy of continuous improvement in the organization so that an environment is created in which each individual is committed to seeking ways of enhancing performance?
6. Are levels of quality measured on a regular and systematic basis to ensure that there is a clear focus on facts and data so that necessary improvements can be made?
7. Are determined efforts made to maximize awareness of the importance of quality, and to achieve the commitment of all employees to the improvement of quality by educational, training and communication programmes?
8. Have adequate steps been taken to review the skill needs for all levels within the organization, and to ensure that the recruitment, training and development processes cater for the likely skill needs required to achieve the continuous improvement of quality?

9. Is proper attention paid to quality in the development of products and processes – building quality into the product or service?

10. Is there a senior manager with the necessary authority who is clearly responsible for quality and is expected to coordinate and monitor the quality system and see that prompt and effective action is taken to ensure that quality objectives and standards are met?

11. Have the nature and degree of organization structures, resources, responsibilities, procedures and processes affecting quality been fully documented?

12. Has an integrated approach to quality management been developed which takes account of the interdependencies of different functions and processes in the achievement of total quality?

13. Are there properly documented procedures for measuring quality against specifications?

14. Has a coordinated system been established which ensures the provision of all appropriate documents covering planning, design, packaging, manufacture and inspection of products, as well as procedures which describe how functions are to be controlled, and where and when control should be exercised?

15. Do quality procedures establish at all times when a product has been inspected and approved, has not been inspected, or has been inspected and rejected?

16. Are proper records kept through audit reports, quality assurance systems, statistical quality control etc that customer quality requirements are being met?

17. Have procedures and work instructions, including all customer specifications, been defined in a simple form which covers every phase of manufacture, assembly and installation?

18. Does quality planning include updating quality control techniques and ensuring that there are equipment and personnel capable of carrying out plans and providing for adequate quality records?

19. Is quality improvement fully recognized and rewarded?

20. Have steps been taken to meet the requirements of BS 5750?

20

Customer care

The purpose of an organization, to paraphrase Peter Drucker, is to create and serve customers. Customer care programmes recognize that customer choice is increasingly being determined by the level of service the organization provides for them. They are also based on the understanding that quality and service are the main factors which generate customer loyalty to the product, the brand or the services provided. An enterprise wants to obtain good business from its customers, but it also wants repeat business and this is how it achieves sustainable competitive advantage.

The steps required to develop and implement customer care policies are:

1. conduct research into current arrangements;
2. develop a customer care strategy;
3. provide leadership;
4. achieve commitment to customer service;
5. measure, monitor and take action.

RESEARCH

Customer care strategies should be based on research and analysis aimed at finding out who the customers are, what they expect from the organization and the present levels of service provided.

Who are the customers?

The essence of any customer service strategy is to segment the customers to be served. As James Heskett[1] has written:

A service cannot be all things to all people. Unlike product manufacturers, service organizations can have considerable difficulty in delivering more than one 'product', more than one type or level of service, at one time. Groups or 'segments' of customers must be singled out for a particular service, their needs determined, and a service concept developed that provides a competitive advantage for the server in the eyes of those to be served... Segmentation is the process of identifying groups of customers with enough characteristics in common to make possible the design and presentation of a product or service each group needs.

Segmentation involves identifying each customer or client group, and listing the products and services provided by type, volume and location. The analysis should include not only what is initially provided for each segment, but also the arrangements for after-sales service and follow-up.

Customer expectations

Research into customer expectations aims to establish what levels of service they want from whatever organization is providing the product or service. The research should cover initial service levels, the provision of continuing services and after-sales services. It should cover the levels of service provided by competing organizations, identifying the particular things they do, how well they do them and how their customers react.

Current levels of service

An audit should be made of current service standards. Customer research may include the following approaches listed by Alan Fowler[2]:

- personal interviews with customers by senior managers, seeking views about current standards;
- questionnaires to customers along similar lines;
- analyses of customer complaints;
- senior managers taking spells of duty on reception or enquiry desks to experience direct customer contact;
- for public sector bodies such as local authorities and health authorities, public opinion surveys commissioned from specialist consultancies.

As Alan Fowler points out, the organization's own employees – particularly those in direct contact with customers – are a rich source of information and ideas. They are the people to whom customers first complain if things go wrong. He suggests that employees may be involved in customer research by establishing customer care teams, charged with examining specific aspects of the organization's activities, and reporting their findings and proposals.

STRATEGY

The strategy for customer care should be based on the research, starting with the segmentation and analysis of expectations and the definition of service priorities, and continuing with a definition of service standards in different segments of the business, and the preparation of plans for achieving those standards.

Segmentation

Segmentation can take various forms. Milind Leale and Jagdish Sheth[3], for example, group equipment users into four categories, as follows.

1. Low fixed and low variable costs, eg inexpensive watches, where the strategy might be not to repair the appliance at all but to make it inexpensive enough to replace easily, and reliable enough so that the customer does not need a new one too often, while making the product impossible to repair.
2. Fixed costs high relative to variable costs, eg cars, where reliability is crucial.
3. Variable costs exceed fixed costs, eg earth-moving equipment and business personal computers, where manufacturers have to concentrate on repair teams in the field, efficient spare parts provision, designing products to be repaired quickly and making them on a modular basis so that defective modules can easily be exchanged for good ones.
4. Very high fixed and variable costs, eg in banks which rely on extensive and sophisticated information technology systems, the most effective service strategy will be to design fail-safe equipment with back-up components, and to monitor and maintain the equipment continuously.

Segmenting by customer needs and expectations means that the organization can flex its levels of service according to needs and demands, thus targeting customer care and, incidentally but importantly, avoiding wasteful expenditure in providing inappropriate or unnecessarily high levels of service. The research should have established where the priorities should be in developing new or revised service standards in each of these customer segments. It should also indicate what changes need to be made to existing customer care policies, procedures and facilities.

Service standards

Service standards can be set in both quantitative and qualitative terms, bearing in mind that qualitative reality is just as important as quantitative precision.

Quantitative standards cover such areas as:

- time taken to process orders;
- speed of response to enquiries or complaints;
- number of complaints, or the ratio of complaints to the number of customers, transactions or servicings;
- number and type of defects identified after sale;
- statistical analysis of responses to customer questionnaires.

Qualitative standards include the way in which customers are treated – either at the point of sale or when they are returning goods or complaining, the manner in which personal or telephone callers are dealt with and the content and tone of communications with customers.

Plans

Plans for developing customer care programmes should cover:

- who is to be responsible – the overall responsibility must rest with top management but it is highly desirable to designate a senior executive as the 'director of customer care' and provide them with the required support in conducting research and analysis, training staff and evaluating performance – it is often helpful to have a customer care project team comprising management members from the sales, distribution and service functions, and employee representatives;
- the introduction of new facilities and procedures for handling customers, eg an on-line computer system which gives customer service staff immediate access to customers' records so that they can answer queries without delay;
- education and training programmes;

■ methods of monitoring service levels, and revising standards and procedures as required.

LEADERSHIP

Definition of customer care standards, and measurement and control mechanisms are not enough. They have to be underpinned by a service-oriented culture, which is essentially the values, beliefs and norms about customer care which are shared by people in the organization. A positive culture will be shaped by the organization's leaders – by the way they act and the example they set, as well as by what they say. It is deeds not words that count and exhortation is not enough.

Leadership is required to make the customer care strategy a day-to-day reality. It means articulating requirements, setting standards, following-up whenever required and getting involved in significant customer care issues which affect the achievement of the strategy.

ACHIEVING COMMITMENT

Commitment to customer care is provided by leadership but also, importantly, by training and communication programmes and by relating rewards to the achievement of standards.

Training

Training in customer care should cover:

■ general customer awareness courses for staff at all levels in the organization;
■ the development of the specific skills and behaviours required to achieve customer care standards – these will include responding to requests and handling complaints;
■ how to operate any new systems designed to improve customer care, such as a simpler order and delivery procedure;
■ how reception and first-contact staff should behave so as to display a welcoming and helpful manner.

Training should be given by people actually involved in customer care. On courses, maximum use should be made of videos and role plays. But the most effective training will take place on-the-job, where employees can learn from the example set by more experienced staff and their managers, and the latter can provide help in the form of coaching and counselling as required.

Performance management

Performance management processes (see Chapter 17) should be used to define and agree skills and competence requirements and performance standards in the customer care aspects of jobs. These should be used as the basis for performance reviews to indicate training needs, rewards or areas for improvement. Rewards can be both financial and non-financial; recognition and praise as well as performance-related or skill-based pay.

MONITOR AND TAKE ACTION

Customer care performance needs to be monitored continuously against both quantitative and qualitative standards. This can be carried out by audits, questionnaires and surveys as well as by the performance management process.

Ten criteria for customer care

1. The drive for customer care must be led from the top.
2. Customer care must be accepted and 'owned' by management at all levels as something which will lead to specific and measurable improvements in organizational performance and overall effectiveness.
3. Actions speak louder than words. Anything that management does which affects customer service, however remotely (and this means just about everything), should be seen by all concerned as part of a continuous improvement process.
4. The concept of customer care and all that it implies must be spread to all levels of the organization. A 'cascade' approach is usually best if it generates commitment and action at each level, which can be passed on down the organization.
5. The approach to developing constructive, positive and profitable attitudes towards customer care must make the customer come alive for all employees. This involves making the points as strongly as possible that 'real people are counting on us to do our jobs well' and that 'every contact with a customer is an opportunity to add value and quality'.

6. All customer links should be explicitly identified and strengthened.

7. All employees should be regarded as customers, so that messages about customer service can be presented to them as real concerns which they have to live with, rather than abstractions such as productivity and profitability. They know when they are getting value as customers and the concept of added value can therefore easily be made real to them.

8. Direct links should be established between what every function does and its impact on the customer. This includes those which are not in direct contact with customers. In fact, particular care should be taken to include them. Having established the links, analyse the attitudes and skills required to provide better customer care and assess the degree to which the attitudes exist and the skills are practised. Any gaps identified between actual and desired behaviour define a training need.

9. It should be remembered that doing things better generally means doing things differently. Improving levels of customer service involves cultural change. This is not achieved easily or quickly. One or two-day seminars and a lot of sloganizing are not enough. Continuing effort is required to produce commitment to customer care, and to make significant changes for the better in attitudes and behaviour.

10. The impact of customer care on performance, and on customer attitudes and buying behaviour must be measured. Success criteria should be set and results monitored against these criteria in direct bottom-line terms or by means of customer research and attitude surveys.

CONCLUSION

To summarize, the objectives of a customer care programme could be defined as being to achieve:

- an open, participative management style;
- effective communications systems at all levels;
- recognition of colleagues and the public as customers;
- development, implementation and monitoring of performance standards designed to achieve excellence in service, quality and efficiency.

Great emphasis should be placed on defining for each aspect of customer care the success criteria, how performance will be measured and how it will be monitored. These, and the actions required to meet the criteria, are disseminated through a comprehensive training programme.

References

1. Heskett, J (1986) *Managing in the Service Economy*, Harvard Business School Press, Boston, Mass.
2. Fowler, A (1993) 'Implement a customer care scheme', *Personnel Management Plus*, January.
3. Lele, M and Sheth, J (1987) *The Customer is Key*, Wiley, New York.

CUSTOMER CARE CHECKLIST

1. Have customers been segmented according to their service requirements?
2. Have customer expectations about service levels been analysed?
3. Has an audit been carried out of customer care activities, the levels of service achieved and the reactions of customers?
4. Is there a customer care strategy which incorporates customer care standards and plans for achieving them (including a designated person responsible overall for customer care)?
5. Is top management fully committed to customer care?
6. Are the ordering, distribution and service facilities provided by the organization satisfactory from a customer care point of view?
7. Are all employees fully aware of the customer standards they are expected to achieve?
8. Has adequate on and off-the-job training been provided on customer care skills and behaviour?
9. Is performance assessed and rewarded by reference to customer care requirements?
10. Are proper steps taken to measure customer care levels against standards and is swift corrective action taken when necessary?

21

Introducing new technology

The introduction of new technology in the shape of information technology and advanced manufacturing technology is perhaps the most significant lever used by organizations for improving performance. But its impact depends, to a large degree, on the people who have to work with the new technology, and the contribution it makes to increasing organizational effectiveness can be seriously hampered if insufficient attention is paid to the human factors involved.

What are required are well-developed policies and procedures for introducing new technology. These should be established in the light of an analysis of why the new technology is being introduced and what the human implications are.

REASONS FOR INTRODUCING NEW TECHNOLOGY

New technology is introduced to:

- reduce operating costs and improve efficiency;
- increase flexibility and speed of response;
- raise the quality and consistency of products;
- improve control over operational processes.

Cost and efficiency improvements

New technology can lead to reductions in the numbers employed because it provides a substitute for existing workers or facilitates the more economical allocation of work. This arises from the use of such technologies as automated processing, robotics, computer-controlled machine tools (direct numerical control), fully computerized production systems (computer integrated manufacturing) and other information processing systems, eg electronic point-of-sale (EPOS) systems in retailing.

New technologies can also reduce costs by permitting improved stock control, the reduction of waste due to operator error and better plant utilization through computerized scheduling. Advanced manufacturing systems offer a combination of these advantages by integrating the different elements of design, process planning, manufacturing, material handling, storage and stock control.

Flexibility and speed of response

Competitive advantage is often dependent on responding quickly to new sales opportunities. Many firms now have to compete on the basis of offering custom-built products produced in smaller batches and often involving complex machining. Flexibility is therefore essential and this can be achieved with the help of new computer-controlled technology which can run a range of production items through a single facility with the minimum of cost and delay when changing from one specification to another.

On-line computer facilities can provide instant information to finance houses and mail-order firms when dealing with customer applications, requests and enquiries.

Quality

Quality can be improved by the use of robotics, computerized process control or electronic monitoring systems.

Control information

On-line information can be made available to managers for control purposes, thus speeding up decisions and eliminating the need for intermediary people to interpret and relay the control information. EPOS systems are a good example of this process. By capturing data through the scanning of bar-coded items they can transmit information of sales and stocks directly to store managers, and central buying and distribution departments.

IMPACT OF NEW TECHNOLOGY ON PEOPLE

The most significant areas in which new technology can impact on people are:

■ the need to acquire new skills and, in many instances such as cellular manufacturing systems, an extended range of skills (multiskilling);
■ skills redundancy – old skills no longer needed;
■ the requirement to operate more flexibly in response to rapid changes in operations and the receipt of immediate control data;
■ the reduction in the amount of routine work and the use of the 'knowledge worker' who controls operations through IT systems;
■ loss of jobs – operators, clerical staff, supervisors and middle managers.

Thus new technology can provide people with opportunities to extend their range of skills and widen their responsibilities (and be rewarded accordingly), as well as leading to redundancies and, sometimes, to deskilling.

However, even when the impact of new technology is largely beneficial to employees, it can result in major changes to their working lives and it will be regarded with suspicion by many workers.

PLANNING FOR THE INTRODUCTION OF NEW TECHNOLOGY

It is essential at the design stage to consider the human implications of the new technology. The aims should be to develop and apply technology so that it will enhance the work environment, and to explore ways to accommodate both the technology and the needs of the workers for interest and involvement – systems designs which attempt to minimize the necessity for operator involvement will produce an environment of alternating boredom and pressure, neither of which will be conducive to obtaining an effective contribution from the worker. This is in accordance with the socio-technical theory of organizations which emphasizes the fact that in any system the technical or task aspects will be inter-related with the human or social aspects. The effectiveness of the technical system will depend upon the ability of the social system to cope with the impact on the people who are working with the technology.

It is therefore essential at an early stage in the design process to explore the human implications; these will include the need for new or extra skills, the deskilling of jobs and potential redundancies.

Consideration should then be given to training requirements – one of the main reasons for the failure of new technology to produce the benefits expected is that insufficient attention has been paid at an early stage in the design and development processes to training and retraining needs. Too often it is left until the last minute.

Finally, and importantly, it is necessary to plan the programme of change management, taking into account the principles of managing change set out in Chapter 7. This is mainly a matter of communication and involvement. Those affected need to be informed at the earliest stage of the plans for new technology, how they will be affected by them and the steps that will be taken to train or retrain, to redeploy and to handle any situations where no alternative work will be available for displaced employees. The aim, of course, will be to absorb surpluses as far as possible by natural wastage or voluntary redundancies.

The greater the extent to which employees can be involved in the project the better. They will be able to contribute their own practical knowledge and it will provide a useful learning experience for them. If they help to create the system they are more likely to 'own' it when it is finally installed.

If employees are represented by trade unions it will be necessary to go through a process of joint consultation. A new technology agreement may already exist which will set out the procedures to be followed, but it may not be easy to reach agreement on more controversial aspects such as possible redundancies.

Even where there are no trade unions, there is much to be said for having a new technology policy which has been discussed with staff representatives or groups and is communicated to all employees. The main provisions of a typical new technology policy are set out below.

NEW TECHNOLOGY POLICY

1. The company is committed to the introduction of new technology wherever this is cost-effective, ie benefits the firm in general and provides an appropriate return on investments, and in particular furthers the firm's need to improve profitability, productivity or the level of customer service.

2. The company appreciates that the introduction of new technology is a matter of concern to its staff from the point of view of changes in work and skill requirements, and future security of employment.
3. Recognizing this concern, the company undertakes to consult with staff on programmes for developing new technology. The reasons for introducing it will be explained, as well as its benefits.
4. The consultation process will include discussions on the implications of new technology to staff. Joint consideration will be given to training or retraining needs and policies for redeployment where this is necessary.
5. The company will use its best endeavours to avoid involuntary redundancy as a result of new technology. To this end, it undertakes to plan its introduction well ahead and to take full account during this planning process of the implications for staff. If, as a result of these plans, any surpluses are forecast, steps will be taken to absorb these as far as possible by redeployment, retraining or natural wastage.

INTRODUCING NEW TECHNOLOGY CHECKLIST

1. Has full consideration been given to human aspects in designing the system?
2. What are the human and social implications of the new technology from the point of view of:

   — new skills required
   — multiskilling requirements
   — deskilling of existing jobs
   — training or retraining needs
   — the elimination of existing jobs?

3. What is the capacity of management to change and adapt to the requirements of the new technology?
4. What is the capacity of those employed at all levels and in all occupations, likely to be affected by the new technology to learn new and relevant skills and competences?
5. To what extent will it be possible to train, retrain or redeploy employees affected by the new technology?
6. How many employees are likely to be surplus to requirements because they cannot be trained, retrained or redeployed?

7. To what extent can such surpluses be absorbed by natural wastage?
8. If some redundancies are inevitable, how will they be handled?
9. What is the employee relations climate in the organization?
10. Is there a new technology policy or agreement covering consultation, training, retraining, redeployment and the steps to be taken to deal with involuntary redundancy? If not, should such a policy be drawn up and agreed?
11. Have steps been taken to brief staff in advance on the plans for introducing new technology, their implications and how these implications will be dealt with?
12. Have steps been taken to involve staff in planning and implementing the new technology?

22

Improving organizational effectiveness – the human resource management way

Ultimately, an organization's effectiveness depends on the quality, motivation and commitment of its human resources. To respond to this, the concept of human resource management (HRM) has been developed as a philosophy and a set of approaches and processes, as described in this chapter.

DEFINITION OF HRM

Human resource management can broadly be defined as a strategic and coherent approach to the management of an organization's most valued assets – the people working there who individually and collectively contribute to the achievement of its objectives for sustainable competitive advantage.

As described by Beer et al[1]: 'Human resource management involves all management decisions and actions that affect the relationship between the organization and employees – its human resources.'

A further definition is provided by Pettigrew and Whipp[2], who suggest that: 'Human resource management relates to the total set of knowledge, skills and attitudes that firms need to compete. It involves concern for and action in the management of people, including: selection, training and development, employee relations and compensation. Such actions may be bound together by the creation of an HRM philosophy.'

Therefore, the emphasis is, first, on the interests of management, secondly on adopting a strategic approach, third on obtaining added value from people by the processes of human resource development and performance management, and finally, on gaining their commitment to the objectives and values of the organization.

HRM PHILOSOPHY

The influential Harvard School, as represented by Beer and Spector[3], expressed the philosophy of HRM as follows:

> We believe that a set of basic assumptions can be identified that underlie the policies that we have observed to be part of the HRM transformation. The new assumptions are:
>
> ■ proactive system-wide interventions, with emphasis on fit, linking HRM with strategic planning and cultural change;
> ■ people are social capital capable of development;
> ■ coincidence of interest between stakeholders can be developed;
> ■ power equalization is sought for trust and collaboration;
> ■ open channels of communication to build trust and commitment;
> ■ goal orientation;
> ■ participation and informed choice.

Walton[4], also of Harvard, developed the concept of mutuality:

> The new HRM model is composed of policies that promote mutuality – mutual goals, mutual influence, mutual respect, mutual rewards, mutual responsibility. The theory is that policies of mutuality will elicit commitment which in turn will yield both better economic performance and greater human development.

THE MAIN TENETS OF HRM

Against the background of this philosophy, the main tenets of HRM are concerned with employees as valued assets, the importance of strategy and culture, and the emphasis on commitment rather than compliance.

Employees as valued assets

The fundamental belief underpinning HRM is that sustainable competitive advantage is achieved through people. They should therefore be regarded not as variable costs but as valued assets in which to invest, thus adding to their inherent value.

Strategy and culture are important

Organizational effectiveness can significantly be increased by paying close attention to the development of integrated business and human resource strategies, and by shaping the culture of the organization. A longer term perspective in managing people and in developing an appropriate corporate culture is seen as important. Every aspect of employee management must be integrated with business management and reinforce the desired company culture.

Emphasis on commitment rather than on compliance

The optimum utilization of human resources will be achieved by developing consistent and coherent policies which promote commitment to the organization and unleash the latent creativity and energies of the people who work there, thus leading to enhanced performance. Alan Fowler[5] has suggested that one of the main themes of HRM is that: 'a dominant emphasis on the common interests of employer and employed in the success of the business will release a massive potential of initiative and commitment in the workforce'.

AIMS OF HRM

The aims of HRM are derived directly from the philosophical statements given above. These aims can be summarized as follows:

- to enable management to achieve organizational objectives through its workforce;
- to utilize people to their full capacity and potential;
- to foster commitment from individuals to the success of the company through a quality orientation in their performance and that of the whole organization;
- to integrate human resource policies with business plans and reinforce an appropriate culture or, as necessary, reshape an inappropriate culture;
- to develop a coherent set of personnel and employment policies which jointly reinforce the organization's strategies for matching resources to business needs and improving performance;
- to establish an environment in which the latent creativity and energy of employees will be unleashed;
- to create conditions in which innovation, teamworking and total quality can flourish;

- to encourage willingness to operate flexibly in the interests of the 'adaptive organization' and the pursuit of excellence.

FACTORS AFFECTING THE DEVELOPMENT OF HRM

As a result there has been a marked shift in the language of management and, as David Guest[6] wrote:

> HRM is an attractive option to managements driven by market pressures to seek improved quality, greater flexibility and constant innovation.

The impact of global competition, complexity, technological change and shifts in employee values have affected UK as well as US chief executives, and it has been said by Alan Fowler[5] that 'HRM represents the discovery of personnel management by chief executives'. For years, chairpersons in their annual reports have been paying lip-service to the message 'people are important'. Now, however, competitive pressures from one-culture, high commitment firms and changes in employees' expectations have indicated the need for action instead of words to obtain fuller use of their human resources.

A further factor contributing to the development of HRM was the extended use of micro-processing technology. This has made individual jobs more self-contained, more skilled and more varied. The 1980s saw the emergence of the 'knowledge worker'. Traditional methods of dealing with shop floor and office workers are no longer appropriate.

Within organizations, increased decentralization and devolution of authority have highlighted the fact that line managers have total responsibility for all their resources. They can no longer rely on, for example, industrial relations specialists to bail them out if they get into difficulty with trade unions. This increase in managerial accountability means that they are forced to concentrate on getting added value from their staff. It has therefore created opportunities for them to become more involved in promoting distinct HRM philosophies and approaches.

This concern for maximizing the utilization of their human resources, and the trend towards flatter and more flexible organizations, multiskilling and high-performance workgroups in cellular manufacturing systems, has brought managers into more immediate contact with knowledge workers at all levels and more highly skilled operatives working individually or in teams. The need to maintain close contact has led many managements to change the old practice of only communicating with their workforces through their trade unions. An HRM approach to industrial relations has therefore been developed which involves bypassing the unions and appealing directly to employees. This distinctive HRM philosophy emphasizes the contribution of individuals and is not so concerned with employees collectively.

CHARACTERISTIC FEATURES

The characteristic features of HRM are described below.

Top management driven

HRM is management and business orientated. It is an approach to managing people which is governed by top management's aims for competitive advantage, added value from the full utilization of resources and, ultimately, improved bottom-line performance. Top management sets the direction and requires everyone to be fully committed to the pursuit of organizational goals. But HRM minded chief executives will appreciate that they are responsible for 'articulating the agenda for change', managing the change process and reinforcing or reshaping the culture of the organization, so that it is conducive to the realization of their vision of the future.

Performance and delivery of HRM

The performance and delivery of HRM is a management responsibility, shared among line (operational) managers and those responsible for running service or staff functions. Managers are wholly accountable for making the best use of their resources.

There is a clear distinction between this approach and the established dogma that line managers, as managers of people, are personnel managers in the sense that they are responsible for implementing personnel policies provided for them by the personnel department. This view implies that line managers 'do as they are told' when managing people. HRM states that they do what they believe to be appropriate within the context of top management's HRM policy guidelines. These guidelines may, however, be developed with the advice of the personnel department which will also be charged with the responsibility for monitoring (but not directing) their application.

In many ways, this emphasis on the responsibility of top management and line managers for HRM as a process of managing a valued resource strategically is the most distinctive feature of human resource management.

Strategic fit

David Guest[7] has suggested that the main feature of HRM is not just the capacity to think strategically but a specific view of the strategic direction which should be pursued. He stresses the need for strategic integration or fit which 'refers to the ability of the organization to integrate HRM issues into its strategic plans to ensure that the various aspects of HRM cohere and for line managers to incorporate an HRM perspective into their decision making.'

The concept of strategic fit emphasizes that, as Karen Legge[8] put it: 'Personnel policies are not passively integrated with business strategy, in the sense of flowing from it, but are an integral part of strategy in the sense that they underlie and facilitate the pursuit of a desired strategy.'

Coherence

HRM aims to provide an internally coherent approach with mutually reinforcing initiatives which avoids the piecemeal implementation of unrelated personnel practices (including the latest 'flavour of the month'). It minimizes the danger of treating personnel practices as isolated tasks which are doled out to specialists whose concerns are limited to avoiding obvious problems, and ensuring technical consistency and accuracy within their particular areas of practice.

Strong cultures and values

The importance attached to strong cultures and values is a central feature of HRM. It was as long ago as 1938 when Chester Barnard[9] said that 'the task of leadership is essentially one of shaping values'.

Strong cultures and values are espoused in HRM because they create commitment and mutuality. As Beer and Spector[3] state:

> The values held by top management must, in fact, be considered a key factor in determining whether or not HRM policies and practices can and will be unified...The degree to which respect for individual employees infuses HRM practices is especially crucial. Employees will not continue to be emotionally involved in the affairs of the business if their contributions are not respected by their managers. Similarly,

employees cannot be expected to be actively committed to the organization if the organization does not show its commitment to them.

HRM policies and practices in the fields of resourcing, training, development, performance management, reward, communications and participation can be used to express senior management's preferred organizational values, and can shape the culture of the organization by providing various 'levers for change'. By striving to make these policies and practices integrated and internally consistent, it is hoped that the HRM aims of increasing commitment and mutuality will be achieved.

Attitudinal and behavioural characteristics of employees

HRM can be characterized by an increasing emphasis on the attitudinal and behavioural characteristics of employees. A company adopting an HRM philosophy will aim to recruit and develop employees who will fit in well with the culture of the organization, and whose attitudes and behaviour will support the achievement of corporate objectives. This could be described as the 'hearts and minds' approach or 'behavioural control', and the emphasis, again, is on using selection, training and communication processes to increase commitment.

Employee relations

The more idealistic versions of HRM believe in the creation of trust between management and employees by policies which demonstrate 'respect for the individual' by adopting open, participative and democratic styles of management, and by stressing that employees as well as shareholders, customers and suppliers are stakeholders in the organization.

Organizing principles

As mentioned earlier, HRM evolved in response to environmental pressures which have forced organizations to be more competitive, responsive, flexible and adaptive to change. Organization structures have therefore had to become more focused in the sense that they are shaped to meet the particular needs and features of the business within its changing environment. This has resulted in more decentralization so that operations are closer to the markets they serve. It has involved giving managers more autonomy but also more accountability for the results they achieve through the effective use of resources. Within organizations, roles in management teams and workgroups have become more flexible and rely on people applying a wider range of skills (multiskilling).

The reward system

The reward system can be used as a lever for change to develop a more performance-oriented culture and to encourage the acquisition of new skills. Rewards can be differentiated according to performance (performance-related pay) and competency or skill-based pay structures can be evolved. The reward system is operated more flexibly and is linked to a performance management scheme.

CONCLUSIONS

Human resource management is essentially a business-oriented philosophy concerning the management of people in order to obtain added value from them and thus achieve competitive advantage. It is a philosophy that appeals to managements who are striving to beat off increasing international competition and appreciate that to do this they must invest in human resources as well as in new technology.

References

1. Beer, M, Spector, B, Lawrence, P, Quinn Mills, D and Walton, R (1984) *Managing Human Assets,* The Free Press, New York.
2. Pettigrew, A and Whipp, R (1991) *Managing Change for Competitive Success*, Blackwell, Oxford.
3. Beer, M and Spector, B (1985) 'Corporate transformations in human resource management', in R Walton and P Lawrence (eds), *HRM Trends and Challenges*, Harvard University Press, Boston, Mass.
4. Walton, R (1985) 'From control to commitment', *Harvard Business Review*, March–April.
5. Fowler, A. 'When chief executives discover HRM', *Personnel Management*, January, 1987.
6. Guest, D (1989) 'Human resource management: its implications for industrial relations', in J Storey (ed), *New Perspectives in Human Resource Management*, Routledge, London.
7. Guest, D (1989) 'Personnel and HRM: can you tell the difference?' *Personnel Management*, January.

8. Legge, K (1989) 'Human resource management: a critical analysis', in J Storey (ed), *New Perspectives in Human Resource Management*, Routledge, London.

9. Barnard, C (1938) *The Functions of an Executive*, Harvard University Press, Boston, Mass.

HUMAN RESOURCE MANAGEMENT CHECKLIST

1. Has a coherent HRM strategy been developed which is integrated with the corporate strategy?
2. Do the organization's policies and practices in the fields of resourcing, training, development, performance management, reward, communications and participation express positive values on the part of top management concerning the employment and motivation of employees?
3. Do line managers accept that they are responsible for the performance and delivery of human resource management?
4. Have a mutually supportive and cohesive set of HRM policies been developed to implement the strategy?
5. Are HRM policies directed at developing mutuality?
6. Is the approach to HRM governed by a belief that employees are a valued asset and should be invested in accordingly?
7. Do personnel specialists operate as enablers, ensuring that line managers are able to exercise their responsibility for human resources effectively?
8. Are human resource initiatives in the fields of performance management and reward used as levers for change?
9. Are there comprehensive policies for human resource development which are geared to the achievement of longer term corporate strategies?
10. Do HRM strategies support the achievement of effective teamworking and flexibility?

Index